The Impact of Social Learning

Education and Learning

Dr. Sharon Campbell-Phillips

 pencil

ISBN 978-93-5458-269-1
© Dr. Sharon Campbell-Phillips 2021
Published in India 2021 by Pencil

A brand of

One Point Six Technologies Pvt. Ltd.
123, Building J2, Shram Seva Premises,
Wadala Truck Terminal, Wadala (E)
Mumbai 400037, Maharashtra, INDIA
E connect@thepencilapp.com
W www.thepencilapp.com

DISCLAIMER: *The opinions expressed in this book are those of the authors and do not purport to reflect the views of the Publisher.*

Author biography

My name is Dr. Sharon Campbell-Phillips. I am from Trinidad and Tobago. I am very enthusiastic about community work and the development of others. I am also very passionate about conducting research and writing as it allows me the opportunity to share my knowledge with others and educate them as well as enhance and develop myself.

I am currently employed with the local government of Trinidad and Tobago where I work at the Division of Community Development. This Division is dedicated to developing communities so that persons' standard of living can be enhanced.

My writing career began when I was approached by a classmate from Bangladesh to collaborate and write professionally. I accepted the challenge and we began writing together. When I received my first publication, I was very excited and was motivated to continue writing, I am also a Doctor of Health Sciences

CONTENTS

Chapter One Social Media and Collaborative Learning Chapter Two Social Interaction and Learning Chapter Three Lack of Social Interaction and Academic Stress on tertiary level students   Chapter Four Social Interaction among Teachers and Students Chapter Five Literacy and Social Interaction Chapter Six Social Skills Chapter Seven Social Learning, Cognition and Personal Development Chapter Eight Gender Development Chapter Nine Culture and Community Chapter Ten Learners' Characteristics..... 9

Preface

This book is to engage in the consciousness of the effectiveness of social getting to know, which incorporates online schooling and its impact on getting to know. Training is all people's business and it performs a prime position in our development and it is proper to all people no matter diverse history, culture, belief, and ethnicity. Its miles available and unlimited to each person whether on campuses or online. With the world's rapidly developing populace, many men and women are gravitating towards online applications. Distance schooling has been described through Garrison (1990); Hayes (1990) as no greater than a hodgepodge of ideas and practices taken from conventional classroom settings and imposed on beginners who simply take place to be separated physically from a trainer, and the improvement of latest technology has promoted an amazing growth in distance training, both in the range of college students enrolling and inside the number of universities adding education at a distance to their curriculum. Social isolation may be very traumatic and might cause emotions of loneliness, worry of others, or low vanity. Loss of constant human touch also can cause warfare with the friends the socially isolated character may occasionally talk to or motive issues with circle of relatives' contributors.

Introduction

Education may be very vital to absolutely everyone regardless of their vicinity. each the Western and the Non-Western nation's fee training however they've one of a kind training systems and their training systems are governed by their personal policies and ideas. In both subcultures, training is exceptionally promoted as a foundation of success and they may be both challenged with the lower magnificence and the top class which can every now and then decide the colleges' population.

The reason for the education device in the eastern nations is to instill the belief in students that the field could be very essential and that it surpasses instructional problems that can have an effect on their performances. In Western countries, however, its purpose is to foster innate curiosity in pupils to be able to compete towards each difference in classroom participation.

The techniques between the Western and the non-Western countries each proportion a few variations as well as similarities inside their training systems. 3 variations between the both of them are 1. to permit college students to know that they're all identical and have the same possibility to training, 2. college students and mother and father are completely chargeable for academic failure 3. Students are greater collective-oriented than those of the West.

The Jap schooling gadget encourages college students to research and does not display bias and discrimination; it actually promotes oneness, letting all college students realize that education is for all notwithstanding their differences. This gadget additionally holds each dad and mom and college student responsible for students' instructional failure. consequently, it's far of extreme importance that they both remember the fact that due to the fact training is equally to be had each pupil, it's far expected that they endeavor to be triumphant at all fee. The Western international locations however blame the instructional establishments for college students' instructional failure. This is due to the fact the device is designed for students to compete against each different and be educationally unbiased. also, college students of Japanese are greater collective-orientated; they value the opportunity for group work, as it is critical to them for group-constructing, more suitable verbal exchange and social development, even as those inside the West handiest fee their individuality and independence.

I'm in favor of the jap schooling device. I advocate their perspective on schooling. I accept as true that schooling should now not be confined to a specific institution of humans and that anyone should have the same opportunity to get admission to records and examine. I additionally agree that a training device needs to aim in generating holistically evolved college students, no longer limiting any of them neither showing bias by means of any given imply. While looking for to increase all-round students, additionally it is their social improvement and every factor of their lifestyles. Teamwork may be very crucial to one's development; it enables in enhancing communicational competencies whilst teaching folks to work successfully as a crew player and study the capabilities and techniques to also work independently.

I also can agree at some point that dad and mom and college students are liable for educational failure. I in my view believe that it's miles up to the scholars to analyze or no longer to learn; mastering starts in the mind and as soon as a faculty is targeted at the getting to know outcomes of students, and are dedicated to educating and guiding the scholars, then it's far up to the pupil to take note of their instructional desires. Additionally, determine also performs a vital role in their kids' academic goals; they want to remember that they are their children's first instructor and must not count on instructors by myself to train their children. it's miles a team effort, and one which involves teachers, students, and mother and father. They have to collaborate and make choices and judgments for the benefit of the students. Whilst mother and father work along with teachers, it motivates college students to learn; they feel a feel of really worth and belonging and the feel cared for by way of both their instructors and their dad and mom. This makes students sense as even though they ought to prevail and make their teachers and mother and father proud in preference to disappointing them.

Chapter One Social Media and Collaborative Learning Chapter Two Social Interaction and Learning Chapter Three Lack of Social Interaction and Academic Stress on tertiary level students Chapter Four Social Interaction among Teachers and Students Chapter Five Literacy and Social Interaction Chapter Six Social Skills Chapter Seven Social Learning, Cognition and Personal Development Chapter Eight Gender Development Chapter Nine Culture and Community Chapter Ten Learners' Characteristics

Chapter One

Social Media and Collaborative Learning

Faculties are very crucial inside groups. They are there to present folks with a possibility to research, gain, broaden, and understand. If we do no longer have access to training, we will now not collect the talents and information to enable us to carry out responsibilities which are required people and we gained to be able to effectively speak and interact with others. A faculty is also very essential due to the fact it's far a group that allows us in getting ready to face the demanding situations of the broader world. Attending a school does now not simplest mold us academically, we additionally gain information and social skills which equip us to acquire our goals and aspirations. At maximum mastering establishments, education is deemed as very crucial, and developing properly-rounded students is the college's priority and certainly one of its goals. Primarily based on the perceived final results of students, instructors layout their curriculum in the sort of way that it is going to be mastering-targeted, expertise-focused, and assessment-focused. Via doing so, now not only the scholars will gain, but the communities wherein they reside.

At those institutions, careful attention is paid to the wishes of students and what they possess which includes their belief, their behavior in the direction of mastering, their know-how approximately education and the arena around us, and their talents and talents. A learner-centered environment is one that focuses on the students in place of the teachers, and as a result of teachers being learner's centered; they use diagnostic teaching and the expertise of every pupil to build upon, given that each culture has its one-of-a-kind beliefs. They may be aware that gaining knowledge is past the talents and information which are imparted to college students, however a method that is designed to helping students clear up troubles and make knowledgeable choices. Students are asked to proportion facts about their culture and they may be carefully located by using the academics who are also studying approximately the specific cultures. The practice and the belief of each student are exceedingly respected by way of the lecturers and that they show appreciation for all. Teachers also take into account that the students offer a foundation wherein they are able to make their teaching more correct.

Their environment has to additionally be expertise-focused and each the learner-focused and the information-centered intersect to offer the simplest instructions and skills to college students. This form of environment is one which introduces students to various components of learning which encompass principles and concepts. that is important due to the fact while not having the know-how of every scholar, it'll be nearly impossible for getting to know to take the region and the desires of instructors and the school will not be found out. The information-targeted instructors usually pay close attention to the information they deliver to the students and the kind of sports in which they allow them to participate. the academics come collectively and enforce sports that assist in growing college students while retaining the tips of the school and the discipline.

Additionally, they ought to be evaluation-focused. An evaluation-centered surrounding is one that lets teachers know if college students recognize what's being taught in order that they may be guided. In each study room, the placing is exceptional; but, students are frequently assessed and are given an opportunity to offer comments. This is vital because based totally on such; instructors will then have a few thoughts about their coaching methods and expertise. Remarks additionally permit teachers to revised and check their work and make important modifications. Learner-targeted, understanding-centered, and evaluation-focused instructors right here at this college intersect to supply properly-educated and ready students. While it is crucial for college kids to be assessed, it's similarly critical for teachers to provide feedback on students' work so they may be guided for that reason. College students' works that might be assessed ought to consist of presentation, homework, drafts, and completed studies paper.

Schools have to be like the right haven for students; it offers college students the possibility to specific themselves freely and not be taken as a right. They are welcomed and experience a sense of belonging and have the same opportunity to study as different faculties. All students need to sense critical notwithstanding their tradition, race, gender, and belief. Their objectives to be an exceptional college, therefore; it takes delight in the services which are being presented. It perspectives itself as a network of groups working together to attain a not unusual intention. inside the classrooms, students aren't taught to look each different as a competition, however, as an alternative work collectively and make getting to know a laugh and exciting even as attaining new know-how.

Being a student has great benefits. aside from being properly educated and having the important abilities to carry out responsibilities, they learn to develop confidence, analyze the significance of socialization, the value of teamwork, the effectiveness of training, the energy of records, the blessings of notion, and clearer expertise of the obligation of a network. Mastering acquisition has changed considerably because of instructors enhancing their strategies of coaching and tailoring them to deal with the numerous cultures within the schoolroom.

Despite the intersection of the extraordinary studying environments that objectives to advantage college students, it could have implications. One in all that's the truth of now not pleasant the needs of all students. The desires of every community are exclusive and it's far distinctly impossible to layout materials and instructions to man or woman college students. For this reason, as a trainer, I would permit students to make guidelines and give thoughts that may be carried out so all can benefit.

John Dewey becomes a completely influential logician who had many philosophies that have been used to influence schooling, shape, and enhances the educational machine in many schools. He changed into very involved with the level of education that scholars receive, and so, his philosophies had been geared closer to their holistic development. Three of his philosophies that were used to steer schooling are educational philosophy, social philosophy, and classical philosophy.

In his academic philosophy, he focused on the function of trainers and college students and their studies. He understood that people are real beings and so he developed a fingers-on method with the intention to facilitate getting to know. He strongly agreed that in order for gaining knowledge of to take vicinity, college students' interplay with the surroundings is essential. He emphasized the importance of the collaboration between teachers and college students and the advantages as they examine collectively. This philosophy motivated training by using permitting extra cognizance to be positioned on social reform; he believed that the shaping of society is critical to getting to know and improving students and that it is useful as soon as the expertise and social intelligence, are disbursed fairly amongst all who take part in that society. in this philosophy, on democracy and education (1916) Dewey states that the technique of coaching leads to the purpose of teaching. He stated that coaching and mastering are pedagogical; consequently, the issue matter must be planned efficiently. He additionally warned that the challenge is counted ought to be related to the scholars in an effort to enhance their typical improvement. via his thoughts, he became able to steer the various educational structures to reshape and remodel their technique to schooling in order that learning can be promoted and performed, and in doing so, the schooling targets might be found out.

In Dewey's social philosophy, he made diverse changes to the manner in which coaching and learning are approached. Despite the fact that his teachings were misunderstood for decades, he nonetheless was able to steer training and affect lives positively. His outlook on training to that of the earlier years and become completely opposite prompted activities related to studying inside the study room. He honestly said that curriculum has to be a means of improving students' academic adventure and have to encompass lifestyles capabilities that might be relevant and realistic. He believed that society and network lifestyles play an important role in children's development, consequently, it changed into exceedingly encouraged that the curriculum ought to alter such and that when dealing with troubles touching on the schoolroom, community activists need to be worried, John Dewey. This influences the education machine and lets in for the curriculum to be redesign so that scholars may be higher capable of research from both concept and sensible teachings.

According to Dewey, modifications that occur in society should exist and inevitable due to the fact schooling is constantly changing, and education with philosophy has a near dating due to the fact philosophy is a view of lifestyles that results in the intention of education.

He believed that every philosophy has its specific attitude and outlook on schooling and it's far vital that we enhance children in the sort of way that they can differentiate the diverse perspectives in order to recognize their rights as people, whilst upholding ethical values inside society and the schooling machine. in keeping with the essence of values embedded within the cultural or social background of human values that progressively fashioned through tough work for masses of years and have examined thoughts and beliefs, schooling ought to reap some cultural values and should promote stability in college students' learning. His writings have been used to beautify the mastering and teaching consequences as they had been integrated into the training system.

Dewey believed that the purpose of training is to teach kids how to stay in their surroundings pragmatically. it is of extraordinary importance that children are relaxed within their environment, and that of the school will help to equip the students with the talents and capabilities with a view to putting together them to deal with life is preferred. However, it's similarly critical for teachers to recognize their function in all of this. Dewey believed that schooling ought to be aimed at bringing about alternate inside society and that the school should pay near interest to the modifications so that each toddler's needs need to be met. He also believes that society, through schooling, can make essential modifications using the faculties to decorate getting to know.

Dewey's standards are aligned with the IB education in that they each purpose to broaden students holistically. They are seeking to develop college students with the skills that may be used each inside and out of the study room and to skillfully address the changing global in which we live. These standards encompass concepts as well as sensible teachings and activities that beautify students. For gaining knowledge of and increase to take region, packages and sports have to be trainer/student-centered which permits for interplay among every person involved. It's far crucial for academic structures to take college students' mastering very extreme and their typical improvement. it is just as essential for them to also pay close interest to their abilities and abilities. This needs to be determined in both number one and secondary school curriculum, as developers have to take place from the students' early age.

This needs to be an international motion and not constrained to sure elements of the sector. With Dewey's ideas and that of an IB school, they are able to create effective lecture room surroundings and groups even as empowering their college students. This can bring about active, wise, well-rounded residents for a lifetime.

Social media and studying

Social media creates a platform where students can talk and research from each different. Communication is a written or spoken communique among or more humans and it offers for men and women to talk, inquire and apprehend what goes on around them. Through dialogue, we are able to are capable of talk and study from one another. It aims to convert subculture through creativity.

I believe that after Freire used the time period "dialogue", he was thinking about schooling exercise and how it is able to be liberated. I also accept as true that when he spoke approximately politics, electricity and oppression and schooling get admission to, he intended that energy and politics allow for humans of a certain magnificence to benefit limitless get entry To schooling and educational plans are designed to suit those that are in the top class in society, whereby, if persons are of a decrease class, they may revel in oppression and training could be restrained.

 Freire additionally said that many political and educational plans have failed because their authors designed them in line with their very own personal views of fact, by no means as soon as considering (besides as mere items of their actions) the guys-in-a-scenario to whom their application changed into ostensibly directed.

Communicate is connected to curriculum reform as there

are conversations between stakeholders to lay out a curriculum a good way to create trade while benefitting students and the communities at big. For curriculum to be powerful talk is vital and it should be executed in accordance to the gaining knowledge of objectives.

Speak may be very essential in training and gaining knowledge; it allows for admiration and understanding amongst individuals and encourages verbal exchange. College students also are stakeholders and have to dialogue with the lecturers. Its miles a form of communique that affirms the liberty of people to make modifications and adjustments to situations and records. Communicate needs an approximation in the direction of sports and situations and newbies have the freedom to contribute.

Speak in curriculum reform leads to tremendous studying consequences and creates new mastering paths. so as for choices to be made and for plans to be enforced, communication has to take region. This is where people come together and discuss instructional strategies so that it will bring about wonderful learning outcomes. Freire is convinced that the strength to create and transform, even when thwarted in concrete situations, has a tendency to be reborn. And that rebirth can occur no longer gratuitously, however in and via the struggle for liberation inside the Supersedence of slave hard work with the aid of emancipated hard work which gives zest to lifestyles. Without this faith in people, dialogue is a farce that inevitably degenerates into paternalistic manipulation.

Social media has various effects on the brain and it creates excitement in students as they speak from their numerous places. The brain performs a completely important role in our lives and mastering is completely based upon it, and it allows us to evolve to everything around us. Despite the fact that gaining knowledge is taken into consideration by a physical technique, it is an end result of the connection of mind cells and chemicals. it's miles vital that teachers place top-notch emphasis on the brain and learning that will follow exclusive mind-based strategies to decorate getting to know so that scholars' success will be progressed on the way to allow them to attain their perceived instructional goals.

Brain-based strategies give instructors a unique perspective on teaching and learning and recognition of the usage of the mind's era and know-how to have a successful educational adventure. Whilst those techniques are applied, the scholars' technique toward gaining knowledge may be adjusted and they'll apprehend new facts in a distinct manner. Mind-based totally techniques allow instructors to beautify their teaching strategies and reveal creativity a good way to give them thoughts to design significant training.

Due to the truth that the adolescent brain continues to be growing, extraordinary mind-compatible strategies are required for getting to know.at this degree in children's lives, their brain is at a stage where its growth is experiencing adulthood both cognitively and emotionally. This means as instructors we want to be very conscious of what we gift college students with and how we present it. Consequently, sorting the best techniques is critical to students' gaining knowledge. In the course of college students' adolescent years, due to the method in their mental development, it undergoes a transformation.

Two of the strategies that teachers can use are storytelling and visuals/pics whether or not online or within a study room putting. Storytelling can be real or fictional and need to be age- and revel in-suitable that makes an emotional connection to the target market. Storytelling is known as the coronary heart and soul of training and it's an opportunity to decorate college students' learning. It permits numerous factors of view, histories, private stories, and learning patterns may be used to greatly enhance coaching and mastering. Children have a natural love for tales and it's fantastic how tales create magic and wonders inside the lives of many.

They educate us many stuff approximately life and it enables college students to broaden an appreciation and expertise of the unique cultures even inside the schoolroom. Storytelling also allows children to explore their personal subculture and remember new ideas even as organizing and recording vital matters. Typically, people have a need to share testimonies. Tales additionally permit teachers to research loads approximately their students' cultures, studies, and meaningful relationships, and through the sharing of memories, teachers and children "create the ability for new connections that link them together internal a new story".

it is very important for kids to be engaged in telling tales whether they're factual or fictitious. While children create and inform a tale in their own or a second language, the language turns into theirs. Oral language is a critical device for the cognitive growth of young children. Therefore, using stories within the lecture room can result in more suitable cultural attention. They may be treasured reminders of ways life used to be (in both right and horrific instances), and how they show non-contributors of that culture some of the wondering strategies and beliefs which have made distinctive businesses what they may be nowadays".

Visuals/photographs on the other hand are equally vital within the classroom and the training machine. They're a visible object which might be used to encourage students and promotes getting to know them. Visuals/snapshots attraction to most kids at a greater stage than undeniable textual content and they reply to visual records at a greater rapid tempo than to textual content only substances. Also, visuals help enhance gaining knowledge of fairly and on many exclusive degrees. I believe that visual/photograph aids are the pleasant equipment for making teaching effective and the nice dissemination of expertise. Visuals/pictures have many benefits which consist of assisting to shop facts for an extended duration, simplifying verbal exchange, allows with comprehension, and acts on emotion and power motivation.

Pictures are very important and effective when it comes to storing statistics long-term, and statistics are processed faster via visuals. They also help persons to without problems hold close various concepts, analyze information and actually have better and clearer information of latest information. Visuals/pictures additionally create impressions and unforgettable memories. While images are fascinating, they capture the minds of kids and motivate them to model what they see.

However, the quality of vision is critical and it's becoming for nowadays lecture room and they may be crucial to a hit teaching and getting to know than method-based totally guidance. It is through using particular teaching strategies and getting to know tools that students can be greater successful newcomers. Visuals/snapshots are teaching and studying equipment; whilst they're included in study room reports, college students are better capable of understanding new records and material. With storytelling and visuals/images I do no longer expect and challenges or issues inside the classroom.

Chapter Two

Social Interaction and Learning

Social interaction is very important to our improvement, and it performs a chief function in instructors and college students studying effects. Without it, one will no longer be able to live their complete ability; therefore, it will result in mediocre performance. The term "social interaction" is called a transfer of understanding and the sharing of areas between men and women so that effective conversation and learning may be performed. Although all components of communication are important, face-to-face interaction is most effective and probably the most important, as it an extra advanced socially intricate operation than we realize and allows for humans to express themselves in diverse methods. Because of interplay, human beings are higher able to design policies, choose instructional establishments and if feasible, give ideas approximately systems inside which they stay. Social interplay is a lively grouping of social sports among or greater people who regulate their activities and responses because of activities and their responses because of activities by their interplay colleagues, and social intuitive may be separated into unintentional, repeated, ordinary, and controlled classes. Social interaction also allows students to turn out to be more self-assured and it increases their vanity.

Gagne's nine activities, that is the best healthy, a behaviorist method or a cognitive method as it pertains to mastering. It is crucial to apprehend and know what each of these tactics is. Behaviorism is a philosophy based totally on the proposition that all matters we do - inclusive of, performing, questioning, and feeling can and ought to be regarded as behaviors. In schooling, behaviorist approaches emphasize changing behavior via profitable accurate overall performance. The constructivist psychologies theorize investigates how humans create systems for meaningful expertise in their worlds and experiences. It states that in constructivist procedures the emphasis is on the energetic engagement of newbies with the conceptual content through techniques along with talking, writing, interplay, and hassle solving.

The cognitive-Constructivist technique is used to demonstrate Gagne's nine occasions of guidance. The important thing to a hit gaining knowledge of the use of the cognitive model is satisfactory of processing that takes place while actively attractive with the subject rely on. To explain the 9 events of coaching my lesson may be on Meander and Oxbow Lake formation for year freshmen. Essential to notice here is this institution of college students falls into the group, which Piaget (McLeod, 2018) refers to as Formal Operational degree (11years and older). During this level, novices will broaden the capability to reflect on consideration on abstract principles and could be capable of logically test hypotheses.

Gagne's nine activities of coaching – Meander and Oxbow Lake Formation.

1.   Get the eye of the newcomers.

To seize the inexperienced persons' attention, I'm able to display them one-of-a-kind photos of a rivers' adventure from the beginning to the mouth. freshmen could have the possibility to ask questions and make statements approximately what they see. Questions might be replied to by using fellow students.

2. Inform students of the Lesson goals.
Inform them what they will examine and the way they will be capable of using this knowledge.
- To understand what techniques are found in a meander
- To understand how an oxbow lake is fashioned
With the usage of this expertise, you will be in a position to show (hypothesize) how a river shapes the panorama.

3. Stimulate previous learning.
Construct on what novices already understand. Ask freshmen about their expertise of ideas of preceding lessons.
- Group hobby
Students need to kind photographs of types of erosion and transportation techniques in rivers. They'll want to signify the type of process and write down an explanation of each. (e.g. how does it erode the river and how does it transport eroded materials)

4. Gift the content material.
Display the new content material. Displaying the beginners, the one-of-a-kind levels inside the formation of a meander. Trainer explains the impact of speed and circulates discharge, demonstrating this visually. They need

to make the connections of pace and discharge with erosion and discharge.

5. Offering studying steering.

This will be done by using students using their understanding of river erosion and transportation. They may need to explain how those methods cause a river to meander. This will be carried out using diagrams and can be explained to the rest of the elegance through the companies. Trainer actions around and offer help best to the ones businesses who're moving in the wrong direction.

6. Elicit performance.

Learners observe this newly received know-how and demonstrate their mastering by building a version to show the processes involved and the way the river starts off evolved to meander. Newbies are required no longer handiest to construct the model but should encompass motives of the diverse staged within the improvement of the meander till it sooner or later turns into an oxbow lake.

7. Offer feedback.

Provide on-the-spot feedback on the newcomers' overall performance, reinforcing and correcting errors. the teacher will be taking walks around at the same time as learners are doing the challenge and ask numerous questions to reinforce their studying, direct newbies into the proper route to discover the answers however does no longer offer the best solution. Provide guidelines and guidelines.

8.   Determine performance.

Take a look at to decide to what extent the new know-how has been discovered. A presentation in their models with the accompanying clarification. The usage of a rubric to evaluate this.

9.   Enhance retention and transfer.

Provide comparable hassle scenarios and inspire newcomers to transfer newly obtained knowledge to novel conditions. In the subsequent lesson, we will be looking at river landforms in the lower direction of the river. Learners will want to provide causes on how these landforms in that part of the river.

Self-esteem

Vanity refers back to the evaluative aspect of self-idea. It is the feeling of our self-confidence and the values that end result while the self criticizes and judges itself. Vanity is performed as crucial to our lives and its significance comes from a mental development framework. Understanding it facilitates us to create a balance in our lives and cope with the challenges of life that confront us every day, whilst allowing us to make knowledgeable selections. However, this can simplest be finished if humans consider that they deserve a satisfied and pleasurable existence. when men and women lack the perception and self-assurance, they will capable of carrying out duties and growth outside productiveness, but the inner force to inspire behavior for healthful self-esteem will no longer be a gift, and so, it's going to go away them with starvation and a need with a purpose to cause them to experience not as good as others. It's far commonly acknowledged that exercise is beneficial for bodily and particularly mental health, as exercise raises usual temper. The term vanity is also used to explain someone's universal experience of self-esteem or private price. This tells how a whole lot we respect and like ourselves; while, our snapshots are defined as mental representations of emotional attitudes, ideals, and perceptions of themselves. Shallowness offers beneficial techniques for making existence selections and for addressing difficult obligations. it is an idea that may be implemented to each person because it entails the opinions of someone's attributes, skills, and a measuring device of self-esteem. The manner we see ourselves is a vital factor of growing vanity on the part of someone. it is crucially marked that our perception is also an imposed ideation from the social way of accepting a characterization that signifies how we feel about ourselves, can be therefore the society facilitates to create a photo that is characterized by using a lack of self-belief and poor wondering and feeling about oneself.

Effects of low shallowness

Folks experiencing low shallowness usually experience unimportant, useless, and unloved. According to Rosenberg & Owens (2001), people with low shallowness have a tendency to be hypersensitive and they have a delicate sense of self that can effortlessly be wounded with the aid of others. vanity is closely linked to mood, so when it is at a completely low level, folks might also enjoy poor feelings, unhappiness, self-loathing, disgrace, terrible self-ideals, anxiety, loss of motivation, fear, anger, loneliness, pressure, loss of self-care or even despair. Each person stories intervals of terrible emotions; but a person suffering from low shallowness will have an especially difficult time coping with conditions that confront them. Low shallowness makes folks hate themselves because they usually sense that they're no longer top sufficient for something; they sense that in order for them to be of well worth, they need to be perfect which is not possible. Low vanity additionally makes it difficult for folks to shape relationships. They trust that they may be powerless to alternate situations might also result in fear and anxiety, and whilst compounded through the notion that their own mind doesn't depend on others, it'll deepen their repressed hurt and anger. When you have low self-esteem, you become a "human's pleaser". You do no longer have clear obstacles and you as in case you are unable to mention an item to something which you aren't in settlement with. You feel unworthy of receiving goodness from others and also you feel obligated to ensure others feel top so that you will just do as you're told and say yes to the whole thing you're asked to do or to agree really worth.

Effects of excessive shallowness
Having high self-esteem has many benefits and it performs an important function in every wonderful experience in one's lifestyle. It helps individuals to look superb in each state of affairs despite how challenging or complex and allows persons to cope with adversity and to absolutely admire the experience. In this speedy-paced society that we stay in, there's usually someone or something demanding a while and interest. However, while we've got a high vanity,

we feel self-confident, purposeful, and self-influenced. With excessive self-esteem, complaint loosens its maintain; whilst folks criticize something you did, you don't get upset but instead, use it as a getting-to-know tool to do higher. Strain will become more plausible; when confronted with stress, by means of having an effective outlook on things, you'll be capable of control it extra effectively. Folks can express themselves extra simply and without worry; having high shallowness permits folks to specific themselves the manner they want no matter how others feel about it. They have confidence and self-ideals and that they consider in themselves and their views. Relationships are more healthy; due to the perceptions of persons with high vanity, they're able to construct healthy relationships with others, and Setbacks do not preserve them down; they keep in mind that in existence there will be setbacks and that some setback has effective consequences. In addition, they keep in mind that the whole thing takes place for a motive and now and again you simply need to believe the manner and consider that the results could be positives. With excessive vanity, folks treat themselves better and they're more privy to what they do and do not need in existence, making them more organized to articulate their feelings. they're additionally extra aware of relationships that are toxic, as opposed to uplifting, and are better geared up to put off themselves if required.

Vanity is something that we carry all of the time be it positive or negative. Consistent with Mead (1934), symbolic interactionism, self-esteem is a system wherein people respond to themselves depending on the attitudes of the primary figures in their lives. As such, low self-esteem develops while individuals are devalued or rejected via these most important figures surrounding them. it's far hooked up that individuals with high shallowness perceived social recognition, even after having been personally rejected by using their friends, therefore, high vanity is viewed as something that each character must aspire to have. Conversely, low vanity people perceived social rejection even after being informed they have been in my view common. Here we see that excessive and occasional self-esteem human beings are seen as similarly likable under neutral conditions. We are able to touch it, but it affects the manner we feel. We can't see it; but, it's miles there when we look inside the reflection. We will hear it, however, it's far there whenever we speak about ourselves. It's far an important but mysterious issue; it's miles our shallowness! It's far the confidence in our very own merit as people.

Teachers' position in elegance organization

Teachers play a huge role in retaining the class prepared, centered, and academically engaged. Trainer desires to establish and preserve getting to know the environment in orderly manners to boom meaningful studying engagement, to save you, and to control terrible behaviors in addition to facilitate social and emotional boom of the scholars. Social-ecological setting wherein college students characteristic can have an effect on their attitudes and moods, their behavior and performance, their self-concept, and trendy feel of well-being. Implementing agreement, rules, and methods, not simplest ensures a secure and at ease gaining knowledge of environment but significantly maximizing mastering possibilities. Effective lecture room management techniques encompass (1) writing magnificence promise, (2) organizing general study room regulations and techniques, and (three) consistently reinforcing norms. It means college students and teachers are actively taking part and participate to create elegant settlements to set up trendy regulations and approaches. The possibility is given to college students to study and expand their complete being as a nicely-rounded person creates a robust emphasis on addressing student's wishes and empowering their lively participation.

There may be a want to spotlight students' ownership towards their studying via offering opportunity for them to broaden and allowing them to decide their gaining knowledge of the method and direct their studying dreams, which include the way they set their anticipated conduct and remedy behavior, and it needs to be gift a big variety of regulations and approaches in the faculty and within the study room too. If the teacher is regular with strategies and rules the schoolroom environment might be superb, the scholars realize what is going to be assumed during all of the year. "Students want an interesting, stimulating, and enriching learning surroundings to develop and thrive. with a view to gain this sort of wealthy environment, effective instructors set up and talk tips for expected behavior, display student behavior, hold college students on a mission, and infuse humor, care, and admire into the lecture room interactions, on the way to increase a climate that is conducive to a student studying." because of it a high quality gaining knowledge of environment can shape scholar results in cognitive, motivational, emotional, and behavioral domain names. Others, the attributes of worrying, supportive, secure, difficult, and academically robust help outline what it method to have tremendous learning surrounding this is conducive to pupil success. However, it may be defined, that all teachers and directors, and even students, themselves, apprehend how treasured a wonderful lecture room climate is to analyze. The maximum customary criteria used to outline getting to know environments are probably the physical association of the schoolroom, area, and workouts, employer of gaining knowledge of activities, and the engagement of college students with responsibilities, amongst others.

If we do now not have a routine in the study room, even in a flexible classroom discipline we have a tough work to attain high-quality classroom surroundings. Policies and tactics have to be encouraged and discouraged through teachers, management, and students too. While college students are becoming a routine in their educational existence, they receive in a high-quality way the brand new procedure. Growing effective classroom surroundings for college students it's one of the core standards in the faculty, due to the fact, when students enjoy being a member of the class, "they're certainly willing to comply with rules. They want to comply with instructors due to the fact the learning revel in teacher offers is so much better than whiling away in time-out." It makes the selection of the following policies and processes a smooth one. Tons of that entertainment comes from their character, their kindness, and the instructor's ability to create compelling training. However, it also comes from teacher's consistency. It comes from instructor dedication to implement effects each time a student misbehaves. However, there is an extra aspect teachers can do to inspire their college students to observe regulations. It's something that in the beginning look seems obvious, but many teachers fail to do. It's a method that may imply the difference between a reluctance to observe rules and a desire to follow them. It's essential to give an explanation for why regulations exist and Dr. Robert Cialdini describes a famous experiment by using Harvard psychologist Ellen Langer, "demonstrating that after we ask someone to do something or now not do something, and the reaction is extra favorable whilst we deliver them a cause. in reality including the word "due to the fact" makes people much more likely to do what we need. This underscores the significance of emphasizing the proper purpose of a classroom control plan, which is to shield students' right to research and enjoy school." whilst teacher make it approximately them and give an explanation for that rules are in the region for his or her advantage, it is able to remodel their mindset closer to the bounds established for the magnificence and teacher function enforcing them.

If instructors and management desire the policies and tactics to be implemented, Consistency must exist. In a manner that teachers will do what they say students will do. Teachers will want to give an explanation for in element how each rule benefits students. It should be this sort of factor of emphasis that at any time at some point of the year they will be able to repeat lower back to the teacher how each rule makes the schoolroom a better, extra exciting place to learn. The instructor has to additionally remind the elegance regularly that once he or she enforces a consequence, it's no longer non-public. "It's not a means of revenge or a way to explicit trainer anger.

It's sincerely a manner to make sure a mastering surrounding that is exceptional for them and their training." (Cialdini, R) "this is one purpose why smart lecture room control (SCM) stresses the significance of implementing results without lecturing, scolding or inflicting friction with students. It similarly reinforces the idea that the whole enterprise, the entire factor of being in college, is ready for them and their destiny. It's now not approximately teachers. this is a remarkably powerful method to introducing instructor who has present throughout all his/her instructional lifestyles to keep tremendous classroom surroundings by means of implementing rules and strategies via way of it turned into description earlier than, can check it. How? Reading the wide variety of queues by friends and teachers, the person and group work how they work, the effects of every evaluation and term grades, their extracurricular work, how is their contribution in the social and circle of relatives faculty surroundings. studying these elements and others that occur in accordance with the precise second, it is feasible to say if the magnificence achieves a tremendous or bad classroom environment by using implementing "precise "rules and methods.

College students had been attending college and receiving training in the classroom over masses of years. Through records, the method of training has changed and it is now time for educators to examine training as a device for the future. To try this, teachers need to take education to the next stage and permit college students to take a lively role in what's being taught as well as how they research. That is done by way of enforcing a progressive instructional version in the lecture room.

Vital idea and social reconstruction is a progressive academic model that specializes in student-based mastering this is relevant to society as an entire. In the instructional Philosophies Definitions and contrast Chart (2006), it claims that "for social Reconstructionist and critical theorists, curriculum specializes in student enjoy and taking social movement on actual problems, inclusive of violence, starvation, worldwide terrorism, inflation, and inequality. Strategies for coping with arguable issues (especially in social research and literature), inquiry, communication, and more than one perspective are the focal point. Community-based studying and bringing the arena into the lecture room are also strategies"

Students are connected globally through modern-day technology. This allows college students the potential to collaborate internationally and cope with social inequality.

One academic theorist, George Counts, believed that scholars ought to construct a stronger democratic society. Counts believed that scholars must "mission every other and build our lecture room network in a way that fosters a lifelong choice to make the sector we stay in a higher region". This could be carried out thru multiple strategies which include community-based gaining knowledge of, crucial thinking, inquiry, a couple of views, and growing The progressive version of Social Reconstructionism and Critical Theorists sell equality within the lecture room through discussion.

All of these strategies can be accomplished inside the schoolroom with the trainer as a manual. instead of having a trainer in front lecturing to college students at the same time as they take notes and memorize, college students create an open dialogue on what's occurring in cutting-edge society and approaches to unite the sector as an entire. Faculties have extra than an obligation to transmit expertise; they have got a venture to transform society as well. Reconstructionists use essential questioning talents, inquiry, question-asking, and the taking of action as teaching techniques. College students discover ways to take care of controversy and to apprehend multiple views". As an example, the teacher can have guided questions posted on the board. The magnificence can be divided into multiple organizations and each organization discusses an assigned guided query. This offers students the energy to take manage the concern in a prepared manner. Students have the ability to collaborate with every different, problem clear up, and use critical thinking abilities. Once students have had time to discuss the guiding question with their organization, the subject can be taken a step similarly. For example, the guided query can now be turned into an undertaking for the group to work on. This continues collaboration via studies, energetic speak, and connection to actual life experiences. The curriculum holds the simple framework of what the direction is to cowl; but, students have the capacity to make what they may be mastering extra real and precious to themselves. as soon as the venture is entire, students can then gift what they have got done to the elegance. These topics can connect to the outdoor global as well as inside the schoolroom. In step with Lynch (2016), "reconstructionist now not only aim to train technology of trouble solvers, however additionally attempt to identify and accurate many noteworthy social issues that face our country, with diverse targets

The modern version of Social Reconstructionism and essential Theorists consists of racism, pollutants, homelessness, poverty, and violence". That is how college students can connect with the cutting-edge world on a global stage.

These methods which might be utilized within the school room connect with revolutionary education in addition to the worldwide Baccalaureate (IB) principles for college students. inline with IBO (n.d.), its project is to "attention on coaching college students to suppose critically and independently, and a way to inquire with care and logic. The IB prepares college students to succeed in an international where statistics and fiction merge in the information, and where asking the right questions is an important ability so as to allow them to flourish lengthy when they've left our applications". This is precisely the same philosophy as an innovative educational version follows, alongside social Reconstructionism and vital theorists. This philosophy is relevant to how modern instructors educate college students inside the study room. Students aren't remote inside one faculty and one point of view. College students are experiencing education and getting access to information on a global scale. it is imperative that scholars acquire modern-day schooling that embraces modern instructional fashions; in any other case, those college students might be left in the back of inside the darkish a while at the same time as reliving the beyond.

The principle and its concept were decided on for this look in order that it can be carried out in practices starting with the little records on the revolutionary and traditional gadgets. Because of revel in and the shift from traditional to progressive, it's far vital to discuss both to look the difference and cause to want the revolutionary gadget. The conclusion is based totally on enjoyment in the college placing as a conclusion of studies and exercise. The revolutionary training movement starts in the 19th century. The primary cause of this training became to 'educate the "whole child"—that is, to attend to bodily and emotional, as well as intellectual, boom. The faculty was conceived of as a laboratory in which the child changed into to take a lively part—mastering via doing. The principle turned into that an infant learns satisfactorily by way of truly acting obligations associated with studying. Creative and guide arts won significance in the curriculum, and kids had been recommended toward experimentation and impartial questioning.' the main supporter of this concept changed into John Dewey, who shared the concept that 'books are equipment, in preference to the authority. This study makes a specialty of the progressive education gadget and its five traits in element and the discussion is focused on the goals of gaining knowledge of. To collect records for this study, questionnaires, surveys, and interviews were the techniques used. The findings might be used for further research.

Modern training and social interplay on studying
The principle idea of modern schooling has comparable qualities in all settings like: 'Emphasis on learning through doing – hands-on tasks, expeditionary gaining knowledge

of, experiential mastering, integrated curriculum focused on thematic devices, Integration of entrepreneurship in to training, sturdy emphasis on trouble solving and crucial questioning, group work and development of social abilities, knowledge and motion as the desires of mastering in preference to rote information, Collaborative and cooperative learning projects, training for social responsibility and democracy, especially personalized education accounting for each character's personal goals, Integration of network service and carrier-studying projects into the daily curriculum, choice of situation content material through looking forward to invite what skills might be wanted in destiny society, De-emphasis on textbooks in favor of assorted getting to know assets, Emphasis on lifelong gaining knowledge of and social competencies, assessment by using evaluation of infant's initiatives and productions'. The hard part of this mastering is the evaluation. In conventional colleges, the assessment is easy and done by means of pre-designed tests. On this approach, accumulating the data, assessing the overall performance and the results, want to be analytic. 'blended with simulations and gamification, experiential schooling products become a powerhouse of records, which can be used to supply tests outcomes correctly across cognitive mastering, talents have an effect on and goal results. The analytics engines in these practice report, examine and provide an in-depth document on the contributors' interplay at some point of the getting to know.' Experimental getting to know offers lots of techniques to encourage college students to contain inside the mastering process. Use of 'generation and simulations with experiential mastering, institutes are making this concept available each time and anywhere, throughout a couple of gadgets. This has brought the concepts of a flipped lecture room, where the learning is going to the scholars and now not the opposite way'. Social interplay places excessive emphasis on learning by means of movement: palms-on projects, expeditionary studying, and experimental studying. "For the things we have to learn earlier than we will do them, we learn by using doing them."

Aristotle, the Nicomachean Ethics

Studying by Doing is a fingers-on approach to gaining knowledge. The important exercise is the direct interaction with the surroundings to its' full popularity and getting to know. 'I accept as true with that the school needs to constitute gift lifestyles-existence as actual and critical to the child as that which he incorporates on inside the home, within the neighborhood, or at the playground, John Dewey, the academics had been to give actual-existence problems to the children after which manual the scholars to resolve the hassle through imparting them with an arms-on activity to analyze the solution. Cooking and stitching changed into learning at faculty and be habitual. Studying, writing, and math become to be trained inside the everyday path of those exercises. constructing, cooking, and sewing had these schooling additives in it and those sports also represented everyday existence for the scholars," Peggy Hickman'.

In expeditionary getting to know, 'students find out about a topic with the aid of working for a prolonged period to investigate and reply to a complicated question, task, or hassle'. Experimental getting to know based on non-public enjoy and defines as "getting to know through the mirrored image on doing". And the mirrored image is the notice of one's wondering manner and its visibility to others. Its evaluation satisfies the query like "why" and "how" of the learning and continues with the end result. And it additionally helps to reinforce the capacity to analyze. 'critical to this is the principle of the mirrored image as metacognition, in which students are aware of and can describe their questioning in a manner that allows them to "close the gap" between what they know and what they want to examine.

"Reflective newbies assimilate new mastering, relate it to what they already understand, adapt it for their functions, and translate thought into motion. through the years, they expand their creativity, their capacity to suppose critically approximately records and thoughts, and their metacognitive capacity (this is, their capability to think about their questioning)." powerful Pedagogy, the brand new Zealand Curriculum p.34'

This exercise has lots of blessings especially in recent times, as the eye span reduced and interest in training distract different entertainments. Experimental mastering growth scholar's hobby, it maintains them influenced and satisfy their curious minds. They use essential wondering, hassle-fixing, and decision-making skills to accumulate a final result. This approach offers the real-existence enjoy, in which they face many demanding situations and do mistakes. But it offers the possibility to enter the response and study the real scenarios, e.g., cooking training. Allow them to explore the substances, try new thoughts and learn. However, the supplied surroundings must be secure, covered, and right monitored. It enables to keep facts, ideas, and the idea approximately the concern. It permits their mind to procedure it for an entire life. 'Control guru Henry Mintzberg talked about long ago that, "leadership, like swimming, can't be found out through reading approximately it".' It develops the confidence to manipulate, deal with, solve troubles, and educate them to get along with others as well. As their studying notably focuses on the group activities, so collaboration helps to attain the 'ownership of the final results.

Progressivism is the response of the conventional instructional gadget. Conventional training is primarily based on teachers' shipping of data to the scholars thru the pre-designed text-primarily based curriculum. It centered on fundamental education of middle topics like mathematics, analyzing, writing, and so on. It isn't always pupil-focused and doesn't aware of their hobby. however it has the following traits: '1) it is absolutely effective, i.e. the kid learns all he/she desires to understand to become a functioning grownup; 2) although the schooling involves harsh trials and ordeals, each toddler who survives them is allowed to "graduate"; 3) the value of training (e.g. paying masters and non-secular leaders) isn't always prohibitive, and 4) children are not definitely withdrawn from the staff'. However, modern training nevertheless practiced within the international institutes, however with a few versions

Incorporated curriculum centered on thematic units
A thematic unit is a powerful curriculum technique to aid in the improvement of thoughts and openness to the horizon of standards, minds, and thoughts of college

students, trainers, and mother and father. on this approach, the curriculum is designed and organized in step with the principle topic, in thoughts. 'In other phrases, it's a sequence of training that combine subjects across the curriculum, including math, analyzing, social studies, science, language arts, etc. that each one tie into the main subject matter of the unit'. All the sports planned and designed in line with the thematic concept. And that subject goes for weeks in practice by using the trainer and students within the classroom. Many one-of-a-kind subjects may be part of the exercise like several unique US, animals, unique holidays, way of life, traditions, earth, sun device, etc. The thematic unit increases the scholar's interest in the studies, they attain higher know-how and connections between the topic and real-life practices. It covers lots of subjects and topics so, continues the student engaged. And teachers can compact the curriculum and plan lots of assessment techniques. The rule followed to put together the lesson entails 1)' subject matter based totally on not unusual core schooling primarily based on student hobby. 2) Theme ought to be grade-suitable. 3) Objective to grasp in the course of learning. 4) Planned the fabric used for the subject. 5) Choice of sports outside the curriculum. 6) Create the dialogue; encompass a question and answers to stimulate college students' thinking procedure. 7) Recollect version in books to correlate with the activities and primary theme of the unit. Inside the ultimate, an assessment will offer facts concerning conceiving the information of the unit. This student needs to be revealed during the exercise. Thematic units create an extremely good curriculum and it's far very tough for the teacher particularly. It makes instructors rethink the topic and work on it, so students get the clean imaginative, and prescient of the entire unit. I practiced it in my elegance; absolute confidence, it takes masses of time and preparation to put in force within the lecture room. However, its outcome becomes enjoyable. The involvement, participation, and excitement of college students, clean the vision of the complete practiced unit.

Integration of entrepreneurship into schooling

Integrating entrepreneurship method,' making students more innovative, possibility oriented, proactive and revolutionary, adhering to a wide definition of entrepreneurship applicable to all walks in existence'. College students must train their ability and willingly create cost and admiration for different human beings. This concept is the middle of entrepreneurship and is also competence that every one human wants to grow to be the society, irrespective of any type of differences. This method 'aids college students to suppose out of the container and nurture unconventional competencies and talents. It creates possibilities, guarantees social justice, instills confidence, and stimulates the economy. Entrepreneurship training is a lifelong getting to know the process, beginning as early as essential faculty and progressing thru all degrees of education, along with personal training. Introducing young kids to entrepreneurship develops their initiative and helps them to be greater innovative and self-assured in anything they adopt and to act in a socially accountable manner. There are numerous approaches entrepreneurship classes may be incorporated into the faculty curriculum.' commercial enterprise, language artwork, wondering capabilities,

Imagining, and thinking talents can be part of the curriculum. They are able to exercise reliable interviews with entrepreneurs and reputable letters. They are able to find out about the products and the process of their manufacturing or innovation. They could even use their innovative competencies to provide a product or idea concerning the target market's hobby or provide the debate or modification on the current product. They could research their competing products and advantage records, in this manner, they are able to find out about their competitors' strengths and weaknesses. It's going to inspire them and boom their thinking abilities to work on their venture in a higher way in the constrained resources. This practice opens the door of their creativeness, sharing the idea with the organization can help to expand many possibilities from a distinctive angle. This practice is being used in lots of establishments and it helps to expand self-assurance in students and openness of their minds. It's far especially advocated to be applied within school rooms that allows you to assist in 'teaching entrepreneurship talents via school is a system so that scholars are left free to find many ways to be innovative via it. Instructors should also be furnished tips to manipulate students and help them to foster pleasing surroundings for college kids to develop.'

Sturdy emphasis on problem-solving and vital thinking

Vital wondering originates with the sensing of a hassle. It's an exception of concept operating to solve the hassle and to attain a tentative end that's supported via all to be had records. It's far a method of problem-solving requiring the use of creative insight, highbrow honesty, and sound judgment. It's far from the idea of the approach of scientific inquiry. Citizens must discover ways to think severely about the troubles as it's seeing the need to enhance the high-quality of their learning and desires of education, The curriculum involved in this placing calls for a teacher's demonstration on enhancing the development of essential wondering abilities. It can be done by way of modeling thinking out loud, wondering concerning the topic, developing surroundings to understand the concern, offer facts and motivates them to examine and inspect, and growing the techniques to make use of various equipment to increase important thinking. Surroundings need to be high quality and encouraging to obtain the desired cause. College students' traits and progress in the getting to know method could be determined as a readiness to the openness to suppose seriously. This means nearly, most of the college machines. it ought to be practiced with the practice of inquiries to open their minds, like; 'Describe what you spot/examine in this page? What are the 'hidden' messages? What is lacking from this photograph/analysis? What are my beliefs about this? Why do you agree with this? Whose pastimes are being served / who's advantaged? Whose interests aren't served who's deprived? What desires to alternate and how are you going to contribute to this variation? Then continue with numerous sports, in order to see the challenge with exclusive views.'

Organization work and improvement of social abilities

Getting into college brings masses of challenges especially for people who lack social talents. The willpower of students' interplay with peers in group work is the underlying assumption. 'Its miles usually notion that scholars can cooperate, talk, trouble remedy and work collectively effectively with their friends within a collection. Frequently, educators consider that students recognize a way to engage accurately to fulfill their wishes; that they recognize how to ask for clarification while stressed, how to take turns, the way to explain their questioning and pay attention while others are speaking. Then, closer to the cease in their instructional revel in, they go away with the stop of their academic enjoy, they go away with the expectancy of being able to feature and correctly make a contribution to latest society'. Loss of social talents creates life-lengthy problems. To remedy this trouble, teachers can play an important position in understanding the behaviors and desires of college students. And plan the group sports, so the student receives extra interaction with friends. For this reason, proper teacher's schooling required as nicely so she/he can apprehend the blessings and advantages of organizational learning. And she or he efficaciously implements Johnson's five factors of cooperative gaining knowledge of:' 1. Fantastic interdependence: students work in the direction of a common goal. They fail or be triumphant collectively as an entire group 2. Character responsibility: each pupil within the group is classified for my part. College students research together in order that they carry out better for my part. 3. Face-to-face interplay: students promote every other's studying by means of supporting, assisting, encouraging, and praising each other's efforts to obtain. 4. Social talents: interpersonal and small group skills which include leadership, choice-making, consider-building, communication, and warfare-management, need to study. 5. Group processing: organization participants discuss the effectiveness of the institution. What went nicely, what wishes developed and how nicely they maintained an effective running courting.

Organization sports and social interaction play an important function in the success of a scholar's lifestyle. It develops and complements their social skills. They learn to resolve issues, speak, learn to use various academic gear, and practice numerous strategies to handle the conditions. Get them ready for real-life studies and troubles. At some stage in my coaching exercise, college students are required to work with peers for specific activities and assignments. To boom the gain of studying, they also asked to impeach, answer, share their mind, and mingle in one of these ways to remove their hesitation and boom their self-belief. They encouraged soliciting for help to resolve the confusion.
 College students' mastering will be maximized through the teaching of social abilities inside the classroom. College students will sense safe and assured in sharing their minds and inquiring for help while important. They will be higher equipped with social competencies with the intention to help them have interaction accurately and correctly with others in all conditions. This movement studies helped explore student perceptions and views on social interaction during cooperative institution work. It additionally helped me benefit better information of in which social interplay breakdown can also arise within a collection. This led to my coaching of social talents inside the schoolroom and helped enhance student interaction and cooperation within cooperative group work'.

Expertise and movement because the desires of learning rather than rote know-how

Rote knowledge is a conventional way of getting to know. On this approach, students repeat the textual content to recollections its meaning and context as nicely. However, the proper know-how isn't in cooperate with this method and college students couldn't relate it with their stored information or don't even encouraged to analyze the challenge to get proper expertise. The assessment for this sort of mastering is primarily based on pre-designed assessments. But then again, if the scholar is aware of the concept and features a clean photograph of the issue, they are able to relate to shop statistics in the brain. They don't need to memorize the textual content or given records. Our brain works in the sort of way that it chained one's information to any other and this method enables us to develop new thoughts and thoughts. It maintains the learning process and growth the expertise. The one manner of this sort of getting to know which I use in my practice is visualizing. By way of looking, records remain for a long time consistent with the research. And this approach worked for my college students nearly all the time. In this practice, the examination device additionally doesn't require assessing the progress. Students' typical performance is ideal sufficient to peer the effects.

Getting to know desires to be a transformative method through which students can rework themselves and remodel their environment. For that to manifest, kids ought to be an essential part of their mastering technique. The getting to know have to attend to the children. Meaning the studying process is constructed at the precedent know-how of the students and their way of life,

vision, and enjoyment. So in that technique, students aren't considering as an empty bag to be area but as 1/2 complete glass. In that feel, while a topic is beneath study the notion of the scholars at the situation is first taken into action, and dialogue is undertaken to deal with cautiously their false impression or concept. Preferred pedagogical conceptions characterizing progressivism: the combination of gaining knowledge of, their state of affairs, and socializing dreams. schooling is a manner of non-stop growth that have to proceed in an incorporated way, given the holistic nature of the adaptation technique; desires or wishes are also essential situations for getting to know; therefore, reactions are greatly learned in situations wherein they may be beneficial, or related to actual-existence conditions; sooner or later, adaptation is both an individualizing and socializing process, involving mutual modifications among character goals and social institutions, the goal of education being the development of an incorporated social character. The essence of pedagogical progressivism is, in our opinion, expressed through Dewey (1920) via the concept that evolution exhibits intelligence as the internal organizing element to the experiment. Accordingly, Dewey explains, with Francis Bacon and his successors, a reversal which reasons heralding modernity, motive "and its bodyguard of fashionable notions" performing from then on as "the conservative element, the enslaving thing of the spirit."
Experience is releasing strength. Enjoy method the new, which takes us far from adhering to the past, and famous new records and truths. Faith in revel in does not produce devotion to custom, but dedication to progress. What topics to the functionalist psychology at stake is, as Dewey

likes to say, the continuous reconstruction of the experience - translated pedagogically by using the scholars' war of words with difficult conditions - and this reconstruction is suspended from a running intelligence developed during the difficulty's interactions with the surroundings. The idea of enjoying, concerning a regular change in issues and views, is then inseparable from that of development, accordingly giving its deep meaning to the concept of progressivism in schooling. Instructional progressivism is adverse, for the theoretical motives said, to transmission with the aid of a 3rd celebration, without distinguishing between mechanistic transmissions teachings, basically regarding memorization, and rational or specific, appealing to know-how. A query of priority among "logical" and "mental" is performed out here. Very usually, for psychology rooted in naturalism, common sense is suspended from the mental, at the same time as in assessment, for "rationalist" psychology, logically ends in the psychological, which we advise expanding within the destiny for the next era.

Progressivism is a common response of the conventional academic machine. Traditional schooling encourages the form of shipping this is teacher-centered and it's far based totally on how instructors deliver records to students via a specific text-primarily based curriculum. It's far focused on basic training of center subjects so one can create stability so that it will be of great benefit. The delivery of education to college students is critical and determines fine or terrible consequences. Conventional schools also attention to providing simple instructional practices to decorate studying. Today, instructional alternatives are many and lots of dad and mom are interested in increasing among people of every age. But, many folks are acquainted with the conventional type of lecture room. Although this sort of model is criticized closely by many because of its negative aspects, it does have a few blessings and high-quality gain.

Chapter Three

Lack of Social interaction and Academic Stress on tertiary level students

Social interaction is substantially wanted in order for college kids to perform at their finest level; it's far one of the driving forces behind a successful training and profession. People want every different if you want to develop and come to be and to satisfy their dreams. Whilst it is not present in students' lives, they turn out to be annoyed and the strain turns out to be insufferable; it takes far away from their getting to know the potential and their ability. Social interaction could make a big extraordinary in college students' mastering effects; it makes you greater creative and lets you higher understand the arena wherein we stay and how to make choices, in addition, to make adjustments to accommodate different persons and conditions. It's due to social interplay, many humans were able to excel in lots of areas in their lives and reaching their goals. There are numerous contributing factors to the dearth of social interaction and there are numerous poor results. Academic strain is one of the effects, and it prevents college students from succeeding in their diverse difficulty areas. While this takes place, many students drop out of faculty and resort to a life of crime and delinquency, consequently, ensuing in the growth of social problems inside society.

Academic stress

Stress is considered in specific approaches by every character and method different things to all people. Some human beings understand it as a natural part of life, while others perspectives it as an ugly physical and emotional stimulus. However, stress is defined as a physiological or psychological reaction to inner or outside stressors. Additionally, it also affects how people feel and behave. This concept of strain changed into added to the sector and lifestyles sciences via Hans Selye in 1936, and he defined it as "the non-precise response of the body to any call for exchange" (American Institute of pressure). Pressure is defined because of an extensive range of troubles, due to unique academic structures which include test and examination burden, a demanding direction schedule, and considering destiny plans upon commencement. However, in this study, strain is viewed as a terrible emotional, cognitive, behavioral, and physiological process that occurs as a person attempts to regulate or address stressors.

Pressure is a not unusual emotional or intellectual phase that tertiary level college students enjoy whilst analyzing. Tertiary stage students worry approximately how they perform; the volume of pressures and anxiety they feel within the technique of pursuing their academic profession creates a degree of strain that they create which in go back will have an effect on their academic performances. The sort of stress that they enjoy is referred to as educational strain, which is described by means of Gupta & Khan (1987) as "a mental misery with recognize to some expected frustration associated with instructional failure or maybe a cognizance of opportunity of such failure." Even as the life of a tertiary degree student can be a completely exciting, unforgettable revel in, a few college students come upon an exceptional quantity of strain and pressure to perform at an incredible level. The thought of getting into the arena of higher schooling brings with it a set of emotions among many tertiary-level college students.

Upon entry, it is expected that scholars become scared of the unknown as they task right into a higher level in their academic life. This comes with its very own demanding situations which can make the experience interesting, terrifying and overwhelming, which could bring about both achievement and failure. As get admission to better education will increase, so does the wide variety of students who are academically unprepared and lack self-belief in their capability to prevail. Numerous elements mediate in figuring out whether a pupil's instructional overall performance is undoubtedly or negatively affected. Those factors encompass monetary repute, circle of relatives' issues, transitions, environmental, path workload, and stress. In addition, a few students work both day and night time while attending school, and coping with each may be very worrying which can morph into instructional stress.

Instructional stress amongst students has long been an issue of social studies. A few researchers have diagnosed numerous stressors which include too many assignments, competitions with other college students, screw-ups, and poor relationships with different college students or lecturers. Pressure by means of itself is a complex, dynamic manner that involves the interaction between a character and their life experiences. This concept is similarly increased with the aid of researchers who said that academic strain can be visible as mental and emotional stress or anxiety that happens because of the excruciating demands of college/university lifestyles of scholars. Furthermore, research kingdom that the underlying elements which encompass educational frustration, instructional war, instructional stress, and educational tension are several additives of educational stress. Research conducted indicated that college students' ability to reap their most effective educational performance, can be attributed to various factors like stage of educational diploma, nature, of course, coaching strategies, and securing correct marks within the final exam.

The transition from secondary to tertiary degree is a chief duration in a scholar's lifestyle. The transfer from one educational system to every another is a big difference that may be demanding. Students stumble upon confusion, socially demanding situations, and some degree of strain due to the fact the general public of college students aren't completely organized for the transition to tertiary level education. This transition manner can purpose deterioration in educational performance and growth academic pressure for a pupil as they try to adapt to their new surroundings. Studies observed that transition is demanding for students, and some revel in slight, or profound grief and anxiety. In a few cases, students feel the severe academic strain from their family and buddies to wait for the tertiary group and achieve the highest grades.

Equally important environmental stressors additionally play a role, in how university scholars sense and to perform academically. An environmental trade, publicity to exceptional weather, new language, behavior, and social customs on occasion create pressure for college kids that could have an effect on their instructional performance. Aldwin (2007) indicated that strain can encompass environmental and mental factors, as college students' capacity to adapt to the new surroundings also can create strain. Studies additionally nation that strain among university students, may be an end result of the trade of faculty surroundings to college surroundings, which may additionally motive mental, instructional, and social shock to them. Moreover, they also stated that many students are confronted with new strategies as coaching, educational necessities, a new form of members of the family among college students and colleges, and even new relations amongst college students themselves.

In addition, college students who're reading at tertiary degree are confronted with growing academic demands. College students can without difficulty turn out to be beaten with the workload, taking tests, cut-off dates, feeling excessive pressure to achieve excessive grades, working even as attending instructions. Faced with a variety of instructions, assignments, exams, midterm, and final tests together with different educational tasks to finish, the inflow of academic applications and demands can compel students to work vigorously to make certain that they cover their work within a short time frame. Those overwhelming educational needs can motive college students to worry, experience flustered, and stress approximately their academic performance. No longer extraordinarily, Tertiary level students who are not able to deal with the workload are at a higher risk of experiencing educational pressure. Some college students balance both instructions and work at the same time, which is very disturbing and in turn, creates academic pressure which affects their overall performance academically. College students who're unable to preserve the balance between their extracurricular activities from training, imbalance of educational, social performance, and time management are all related to strain.

Although most people regularly take into account grades while defining instructional overall performance. Saqib and Rehman, (2018), defined educational overall performance as an "instructional purpose this is performed via a pupil, teacher or group finished over a selected time". However, in this study educational overall performance is defined as the extent of getting to know in a specific vicinity of the situation in phrases of know-how, information, ability, and application evaluated inside the shape of check scores and their anticipated GPA for the current semester. The Grade factor common (GPA) is now used by most of the tertiary institutions as a handy precis degree of the academic performance in their students. academic performance is one of the maximum vital considerations among students in a better education degree and this may be illustrated with the aid of (GPA), Aspiras and Aspiras, (2014) used the (GPA) to gather data and measure the educational overall performance of college students. The motive researchers reap college students' GPA is to find out whether the pressure students revel in leaves an impact on their instructional performance.

But, despite all of the poor elements of strain, it allows to create stability and it's far taken into consideration a vital condition in assisting to gain a few levels of fulfillment in a college students' academic existence; pressure acts as a negative predictor of educational performance, and it's miles a tremendous contributor to some students' overall performance. Therefore, this courting among educational pressure and academic overall performance continues to intrigue students and researchers alike.

Pressure is a main contributing thing to many psychological ailments that plague today's society. As results from the American dental association (APA) and American Institute of stress survey in 2014, discovered 73% of people revel in some stage of psychological signs as a result of pressure. Further, outcomes from 2009 revealed that young humans are especially confused because of college stress related to instructional performance.

Educational pressure has grown to be a critical problem among instructional institutions and policymakers because of the growing occurrence of suicides amongst college students throughout the globe. A Lancet said in 2012, revealed that scholars a number of the colleges in Indian located that it is hard to address failure in examinations. country-wide Crime information Bureau (NCRB) revealed that in 2015, the number of student devoted suicides stood at eight,934 because they were depressed approximately failing their exams and the numerous unreported attempts of suicides are likely to be a good deal better.

Suicide charges amongst college-aged college students are

said to be better than they have been, and this changed into described through American university health association information posted in Psychology today. Patel (2016), additionally discovered that scholars, who're incredibly confused, typically have self-defeating thoughts. Negative management abilities amongst college students can be skilled by using college students whilst they're stressed, ensuing in them being incapable of dealing with their workload and consequently, underperforming.

For many teachers, they have high expectancies in their college students in spite of the instructional adventure may be very hard and lots of students can turn out to be harassed. However, while students are careworn, now not handiest they're affected, but it influences their teachers as nicely and the organization at big. Due to instructors' high task demands and students' terrible overall performance, instructors turn out to be negatively affected and revel in pressure and sickness as well. The organization may additionally revel in low enrollment as a result of college students' low pass fees or dropouts.

 The majority of tertiary degree college students locate it extremely hard to finish educational requirements, do seminar displays and memorize what they have learned from each path's content for assessments. With an avalanche of labor to complete within the sort of short period, college students turn out to be academically stressed and could not be able to carry out academically well. in addition, students are confused about activities that might be happening internally and externally that can cripple them in one this manner that they will not be capable of performing at their fullest potential, and with provoking thoughts of how they're academically confused, which also affects their instructional overall performance.

Strain-related elements affecting college students

It is crucial to recognize the various factors affecting students' academic overall performance. Tertiary degree students undergo extraordinary challenges which have a completely huge impact on their lives that would cause them to experience some stage of stress. Acting academically properly is a massive fulfillment for tertiary-level college students because it plays a vital role in the achievement and improvement of younger human beings in society. Bad educational performance on the other hand can result in monetary problems, fitness issues, and much more likely unemployment for college students.

Previous studies carried out located that stress and academic overall performance are substantially correlated. These researchers used the college Undergraduate pressure Scale (CUSS) and students' Grade point common (GPA) to gather records that found out that there is a positive correlation. It also showed there has been a susceptible and bad dating recognized among pressure and academic achievement.

The majority of university students every so often senses harassment approximately their educational performance. The overwhelming burden of educational stress that tertiary stage experience of their pursuit for better training is crucial. As many tertiary-level college students have difficulties adjusting to a giant quantity of the instructional fabric. Research conducted awareness on the effect on the pupil's educational overall performance at secondary faculty degree whereas, Elias, Ping, and Abdullah, (2011) investigated pressure and academic overall performance of undergraduate students. There are several stressors that make contributions to academic pressure and educational overall performance.

Strain construct

The construct of stress represents a vast concept and can be view in different categories. To specify its association with one-of-a-kind domains of existence inclusive of instructional strain, process pressure, and dating strain; the present study discovers the assemble known as educational pressure which, in keeping with Wilks (2008), describes individuals' attitudes and behaviors towards academic-related demands. As the majority of tertiary degree, college students' overall performance is exceptionally affected by a range of things which encompass admission factors, socio-monetary popularity, faculty background, instructional, non-public, and environmental pressure. As a result, these contributing elements preclude student's capacity to carry out academically to their highest capability.

There are several theories created to provide an explanation for the incidence of strain and how extraordinary forms of inner and external stressors might also motive a person's strain level to increase unexpectedly. Hans Selye who is called the daddy of pressure approached it from a biological angle. He stated that a stressor or an occasion that threatens an organism's well-being of organism results in a three-stage physical reaction in alarm is how the body reacts with a "fight-or-flight" stressor. Resistance refers to the frame resists toward the stressor and exhaustion stressors preserve past the frame's ability the resources end up exhausted. However, the theoretical framework on this take a look at is one selected to satisfactory provide an explanation for the hyperlink between stress and overall performance.

To provide an explanation for the phenomenon of strain in relation to overall performance, researchers used Lazarus and Folkman's concept of Cognitive Appraisal. Consistent with this theory, a person's interpretation of a state of affairs, in the long run, impacts the quantity to which the situation is perceived as stressful. Cognitive appraisals are human emotional functioning that may be a completely beneficial way of gaining insight into a person's notion of themselves, their environment, and their ability to deal with disturbing situations. In different phrases, the emphasis is on how a pupil individually measures the level of academic stress they may be experiencing, as well as their skills and alternatives in handling it. Lazarus and Folkman (1984) define coping as a person's efforts to deal with strain. He said that coping is one's ability to "constantly converting cognitive and behavioral efforts to control precisely outside and/or inner needs that are appraised as taxing or exceeding the resources of the character." strain may be visible as an end result from an "imbalance among needs and sources". In this situation the demands are that of workload during the semester that students are challenged with; for instance dealing with exams, assignments, and personal life. Whereas the sources are getting entry to a computer, internet get entry to and time students have to complete those demands.

The theory carries essential principles; those are number

one and secondary appraisal. The primary appraisal determines whether or not the stressor or the scenario is a risk, a task, or a harmless scenario that is within the context of the overall performance or an incentive to achieve a goal. For example, inside the event wherein the student fails in an examination and the view that something so as to purpose destiny harm or lost will lessen the performance of and man or woman. Secondary value determinations involve those feelings associated with managing the stressor. Those emotions that include the stressors will determine whether or not the scholar can accomplish their goals.

The usage of the library to inspire social interplay

An instructor calls for the development of his profession thru various ways in continuous ways. Because the exchange of socio-cultural phenomena and the intervention of various modes of sciences and technology are bringing on new developments of demanding situations which require full-size information and expertise from a part of the teachers to hold abreast with the demographic modifications of the scholars. In this regard, an instructor is a frontrunner additionally who can manually a learner in the proper way as the open resources of knowledge create demanding situations for some of the newbies to select the proper facts and centered readings. The library can declare a concern that could maintain an instructor up to date with the modern-day tendencies of know-how. Library, on this, appreciate, needs to be time befitting to accord all the essential books online and printed. This case study has evaluated the necessity of a library, a virtual up-to-date library, to help teachers elevating continuous professional improvement. A university has been recognized because the tool for a case observation to tie the knot among the ideas of non-stop professional improvement, trainer leader, and a library.

The nature of library use is characterized from di-angles within the context of an academic organization (college, colleges, and so forth.). These di-angles may be referred to as (i) the library used for an instructor and (ii) the library used for a pupil. The title of the look at generates four most important principles as (i) using the library, (ii) continuous professional development, (iii) extension of information, and (iv) trainer leader. As a result, the title and scope of the study limit the analysis of the use of a library from a teacher and for the lecturers. Wenborn (2018) has reviewed the troubles of professional improvement with the help of non-stop, effective use of library due to the fact library accords with multi-dimensional stocks of knowledge of various branches and this variegated understanding is necessarily received by using the professional as they need to serve the freshmen with disseminating expertise even inside the faces of the ever-changing surroundings. Accordingly, an expert desires to conform himself with new information of the ever-converting state of affairs in the arena of knowledge to satiate the taste of the freshmen. They need, consequently, to develop themselves constantly and this idea claims the necessity of library work as stated formerly why and the way library work aids in continuous professional development.

Rupsiene & Sarbaliene (2010) have referred to their paper that 'trainer leadership' is the most crucial phenomenon next to 'coaching'. A trainer chief can efficaciously manual their students in achieving missions and imaginative and prescient of the group and may make them a success in the long run of their destiny life. The expertise has been reshaped as worldwide, the aims and targets of an institution are determined to embody this challenges of presenting without boundary lines competencies to the inexperienced persons. A teacher might also teach their newbies what are the demanding situations and a frontrunner additionally courses their rookies thru the methods so that the novices can face and overcome those globalized sorts of demanding situations. A teacher is a chief while they are able to have an effect on their newbies to believe in this sort of way how the trainer embraces the worldwide demanding situations. Here comes the query of expertise, first-rate, know-how, talent a trainer should have. One of the appropriate methods of achieving this acumen is to be familiar with the dynamic existing mind of the sector and the changing dispositions in the sphere of expertise. The association of a library in an organization with diverse varieties of books, connection with on-line libraries of the world and reputed universities and making wealthy with up to date considerate reading substances can impart a manner of being knowledgeable at the current troubles and dispositions of education and global studentship that an instructor may make use of of their realistic sphere of guiding the beginners.

The preceding literature, therefore, can make interlink a number of the variables of sources of knowledge amassing in an institution, the non-stop improvement of the teachers, and the idea of teacher chief. And that is projected that the role of the library in making a trainer chief through continuous improvement can be deciphered.

But the library access eBook for the lecturers in this targeted university, Jashore authorities women's university, well-known shows that eight teachers a number of the seventy teachers had listed their names who had accrued books with uncommon frequencies. This indicates the academics in this college aren't used to involving themselves in library work and the lecturers who are enlisted debtors of the books aren't ordinary traffic. accordingly, the present problem of this college is to find (i) why the lecturers are reluctant to use the library, (ii) why an opening prevails in the library work as a manner of continuous professional improvement, and (iii) how the library can be linked with the making of trainer leader because the library reflects the photo of the rise and fall of humanity and civilization and a key to growing infinite know-how and civilization. It additionally displays all of the extant works of the evolution of human civilization and information.

The Case

Jashore authorities' girls' college is a district-stage authorities-subsidized college that includes 5,000 college students and seventy instructors and also having nine honor's departments. There is an important library having, six hundred enlisted books. All the lecturers and college students are entitled to use this library to gather substances for coaching and learning. however, there are fifteen shelves in an unmarried room which made the room an awful lot gloomy, soaking, and damp without plenty of ventilation of mild and air. This library can accommodate less than ten visitors' sitting associations at an equal time. A 'Liberation warfare corner' has these days been established at a corner of the library which shortens the distance of the library. Mississippi college Library manual (2020) has imposed that the environment of a library should be inviting and barrier-loose. It needs to make sure right relaxation so that a learner may have the scope of relieving their boredom received through the relentless participation of study room lectures. on this attitude, the library environment of the focused college famous uninviting and non-friendly. It lacks the exceptional of addressing the eye of both the teachers and students having little sitting association and cruel surroundings.

It's miles previously stated that the library of this college accommodates fifteen cabinets wherein one shelf preserves fictions (novels, poetry, books associated with liberation war) written by Bangladeshi writers and all different shelves are full of books related to the university curriculum of the nine honors' departments. It's far not able to address that each department has their seminars wherein they established a nook wherein all of the syllabus associated books in their honors' curriculum had been bought for his or her respective teachers and students. On this view, the collection of the crucial library is overlapping except for fewer collections of fiction on a shelf. A general university library emphasizes both the curriculum and the hobbies. It no longer only prepares the students but additionally creates a human being providing those historic, cultural, social, and global angles of humanity though the library must comply with the limits of age, ethics, and values of the lecturers and the scholars to collect books. In light of the above reference, the library of the central college fails to cope with the interest and taste of the lecturers and newbies as it's far a stock of curriculum-associated materials.

The demography of the 21st century inexperienced persons, in addition to the lecturers, is converting. The inception of facts and generation in each sphere of understanding is an issue of the venture. That is one of the challenges for traditional academic libraries. Paper has been open get entry to and materials have been transformed to the digital model and a teacher can undergo the internet to gather materials and nearly every student of better training possesses an android telephone and a computer. With this converting demography, most of the world's reputed academic in addition to public libraries have transformed to offer resources in combined manners. The library of the twenty-first century accords the Wi-Fi facility, online aid collection, and value facility together with the collections of tough copies of books. For that reason, the rookies who're taking PC and android telephones with them are often journeying libraries for completing a task, making ready notes. The getting to know has turned from silent reading to the social, organization, and shared have a look at. Consequently, the necessity of a library has no longer reduced; as a substitute, the library has become to be an assembly region for instructional functions. The change that desires to be made is to grow the scope of the library and remodel it to cope with the changing traits of the site visitors in academic and public libraries. The targeted college has been previously indicated as a central authority-subsidized university which shows any huge alternate inside the structure or design is based on the allocation from the government price range. The library stays undiscussed issues in those styles of faculties which the conventional look of the library of centered college proves it again. The library has no printing and scanning facility. There prevails no computer or laptop. Here, the possibility of mixed studying (the learning which blends the soft replica and difficult replica of materials) is missing.

The history examination of the case well-known shows that the literature, researchers guard the need of the use of the library for the non-stop expert in addition to educational improvement. And, expert, as well as educational improvement, has direct had an impact on the making of instructor leader. However, history takes a look at the famous that library of the Jashore government girls' college creates a gap. It lacks a congenial surrounding, sufficient stock of educational, non-academic books and it also lacks the arrangement of technical components to address the twenty-first-century challenges of e-mastering.

The character of the exercise of continuous professional development of the teachers

The preceding phase is a trial of digging out the need for an educational library within the context of schooling. Along, the prevailing condition of the instructional library inside the focused university has also been excerpted. Now, the dialogue desires to be moved to spotlight the non-stop professional improvement of the academics, one of the middle ideas of the take a look at. The identity of the paper famous that library is to be utilized by the lecturers because the usage of the library is a part of persevering with improvement.

To start with, instructors' development, instructors' non-stop development were researched, discussed, characterized, and analyzed with pointers through the researchers of various nations on occasion. From the readings of one of the research papers and it's to word that a teacher's continuous improvement is marked with (i) being adaptable with any more recent traits of the academic zone and (ii) the adaptability should produce an advantage to the inexperienced persons so one can address the present socio-cultural perspectives. Accordingly, the term, continuous expert development, has temporal and spatial importance. And, the socio-cultural contexts decide what the abilities are the teachers need to collect to satisfy the taste and need of the newbies of nowadays and tomorrow. Sarowardy & Halder (2019) had carried out a study at the capabilities and understanding the lecturers want for the twenty-first century ICT (information and communique era) primarily based learners via being inspired from the findings of the paper of Halder (2019). Halder (2019) has revealed that a hundred and forty-four million Bangladeshi humans have direct hyperlinks with cell technology and 44% of newcomers of better education rely in large part on nets to make their educational courses geared up. That is the brand new developments and challenges also for the directors, authorities as well as the teachers to make the rookies engaged in school rooms, make the elegance interactive and imaginative. Expertise is thriving; instructional tools and techniques are converting. So, Halder (2019) has recommended converting the coaching methods aside from traditional lecture techniques. In this context of Bangladesh, teachers are the top challenge who needs to be made adapted with the present-day developments of method. Sarowardy & Halder

(2019) have made an investigation on the capability of the lecturers and their aptitude regarding the more recent methodologies of teaching. There, they discovered that out of 12, four teachers are used to adapting newer tendencies of educational perspectives, and their attitude toward receiving education, accepting newer techniques of teaching is poor. The afore-stated references from Halder (2019) and Sarowardy & Halder (2019) clarify the prevailing state of affairs of the schools of Bangladesh. The observed university faces these dire outcomes. Bainbridge et al. (2002) had researched one hundred seventy respondents in Canada and they had concluded that academics are constantly probably to take assist from print media, electronic media, internet, and educational & public libraries to signify books, design, and put in force curriculum. They had the perception that these media may want to assist them to select the excellent assets for the scholars that may serve their instructional reason and fulfill their taste with special attention to gender, age, faith, and lifestyle. Therefore, a teacher being updated paves the manner to get familiar with the updated sources. as a consequence, a trainer can't but be included with digital media, print media in addition to library collections so as to manual the beginners to the proper manner.

It is inevitable that the academic curriculum desires to be modified due to socio-financial-cultural as well as international factors. The educational quarter of Bangladesh has also skilled the changes if we recollect the two decades of examination. Laptop technological know-how had received the topmost precedence inside the inception of the year 2000. The labor marketplace becomes commencing up for Bangladesh in the 1990s whilst vocational and technical schooling become given priority converting the direction of the traditional education of natural sciences, arts, and humanities. Once more, the huge development of information generation commenced a new horizon of getting to know. The curriculum of schooling of Bangladesh underwent adjustments in the 2010s and records and generation subjects changed into determined as a mandatory difficulty for all instructions of instructional degrees. Now, the authority faces that there prevails a substantial degree of concerns on the case of exercising of ethics and morality many of the inexperienced persons of all tiers. Pupil delinquency, price of drug addiction, rip-off, social media misuse, killing of fellow associates, rape are on the upward push of a few of the college students. Now, the national coverage makers are thinking of including ethics and morality research in all levels as a mandatory concern.

Hence, the national, as well as international necessity, impacts the countrywide curriculum. Here lies the necessity of non-stop expert development for the lecturers. Instructors must face all of the demanding situations and they want to be efficient so tackle all challenges. And continuous improvement can make them opportune to analyze each nook of existing in addition to destiny challenges and create them as gifted enough.

The conception of trainer chief inside the case of examine university

The necessity of the management position from the part of the major or head of an academic group is an established concept. The kinds of leadership roles and the need of indicated management sorts in very particular contexts had been set up by way of the instructional researchers as well as the instructional thinkers throughout the globe. Now the concept of transformational management from the part of a college foremost is being discussed at this factor of swiftly changing worldwide situation in the fields of training. Sarowardy et al. (2019) have defended how transformational management nice is required via the primary within the context of the university level training of Bangladesh. It is great here that the flow of a managerial fundamental to the transformational essential is the demand of the day. However, the scope is more increased as it attempts to increase the concept of management unto the teachers in any respect ranges.

Cosenza (2015) has characterized instructor leader in this sort of manner that it isn't handiest the matter of exercising the energy and administering the schools; instead, an instructor becomes a leader if he can affect the behavior and questioning styles of the students. An instructor works on the four walls of lecture rooms. However, an instructor leader revolves beyond the four walls of the college boundary. Cosenza (2015) also retorts that a trainer will become a pacesetter if he is resourceful character and professionally professional, and due to the fact he can assign first-class materials and assist to choose the high-quality manner for the students via his know-how and information. Jashore authorities' girls' university is a nationalized university wherein the curriculum and syllabus are assigned through the central authority of the authorities through the pinnacle-down technique. Then, the lecturers of this form of Bangladesh colleges have little influence on curriculum layout or syllabus training. This can bar a trainer to acquire an understanding within the field of present evolutions in education. This college lacks a counseling center wherein students could have direct interplay with the instructor regarding very personal matters of each the parties. But the possibility of the academics to convert themselves to a pacesetter is little. However this being an honors' stage college consisting of nine honors branches with greater than five thousand students, the lecturers have notable contribution in assigning reference books, guiding for career-oriented arrangements for the activity sectors. As a consequence, every magnificence room is a macro counseling house for both the lecturers and the scholars. This calls for a teacher having much understanding. Information affects abilities and; information may be obtained as well as abilities may be reached if there prevails a good deal of institutional opportunity. The e-learning facility, multimedia facility, ingenious library are a few of these institutional possibilities which the examining university lacks. Hence, trainer management results from non-stop expert improvement, and expert improvement originates from the congenial surroundings and the opportunities that an institution desires to provide to the lecturers. The look at the university reveals that hassle lies in the bodily collection of the imperative library in addition to the university. Again, the agenda of the hole and closing of the central library of this school follows the same as the schedule of the university hour. The 70 teachers are to be involved in taking instructions and performing instructional in addition to administrative tasks for the duration of the college hours and the students have to address a tight timetable of lessons and exams at some stage in the hours. It is a drawback on the part of the university that the library cannot provide instructors a properly pupil pleasant schedule of the use of the library. This could bog down the visitation of the academics to the library for the motive of academic research, and collection of substances for the classes. The middle for research Collections (2020) has dignified timing of establishing and final the library. This library serves 24/7 and it has special arrangements for the scholars as students remain busy with educational duties during the days. This indicates that appropriate timing is an effective signal of an operational and usable library.

Powerful college training

The fourth class of the seventeen categories of SDG (Sustainable improvement goals) is fine education. There, quality training encompasses inclusive development of a scholar's mental, ethical, bodily, behavioral development so that the scholar can grow to be the treasured property for his or her society in addition to the globe. Now, any degree of education can never deny the fact stated as high-quality or powerful schooling. The foremost precedence for an academic organization is to make certain effective schooling that no person can refuse. Now, the focused college for this case observes has a fewer specification which importantly characterizes that (i) the scholars want to pertain competencies-oriented instructions, (ii) they must be made suit for the carrier international within the aggressive global situation, (iii) they need to be made morally residing, (iv) they should be prompted to turn out to be know-how seekers, researchers (v) and they have to be enormously oriented with superior facts generation. the lecturers in these institutions will be organized enough to better serve the scholars and meet all of the demands what a student can count on from these views. Once more, the establishments need to have all requisite arrangements to come up with the money for the teachers with all gear and strategies. Consequently, effective college education turns into a triangular process through which students will sincerely perceive and rightly set their dreams, instructors will manual efficiently thru the manner to fulfillment and the group can have all preparations to meet each the academics and the students. The library helps social and highbrow work by means of bringing human beings and ideas together. It offers instructors and freshmen a touchy area to move out of doors of the study room, for you to have interaction with distinct subjects and have a much wider variety of expertise. Then again, there is no gain to running in Singular. This extensive use of understanding brings forth a component of sustainable understanding that does not exist. The library is an interdisciplinary center as it allows the provision of various facts resources. The take a look at university lacks proper preparations of institutional provisions; like, insufficient library facilities. This deficiency cannot ensure inventive academicians and scholar researchers. The need for the development of the contents of the library is drawing close. This library handiest specializes in the formal, textual, syllabus assigned books which despairs the lecturers in addition to the students to go to the library all the year-round.

Digitized Library paying a good deal

Powerful library way the library from where a learner can

get most of the things and suppose he felt vital at his academic studying procedure. The Virtual Library is a resource with statistics generation that breaks down bodily barriers and makes adjusting for difficult to get admission to. The digital library opens as much as formal gaining knowledge of environments that allow teachers and students to get admission to large equipment and verbal exchange. It combines a ramification of teaching methods. No longer just students or teachers, however beyond formal schooling, the apprentice can interact. The digital library also teaches time, electricity, and knowledge to proportion. Computing generation, worldwide telecommunications also can be taken gain of. it is a limitless array of audio, videotapes. The virtual library teaches us to share high-priced assets. Books, periodicals, software programs, digital databases; strong point gadgets which include projectors, photographs devices,s, and cameras permit customers to proportion. The digital library combines all of the formal, casual, and expert coaching functions. A photocopier device is needed for college kids to photocopy their passages or textual content. This is a deadly hassle for the prevailing observe college library that does not have this gadget together with any gear and strategies so that the sizeable ocean of information turns open to all. The prevailing technology is the age of information and verbal exchange era. Keeping up to date calls for preserving up with modern-day information. However, the components of the facts and communication era require a laptop, internet connection, interlink with various reputed journals in addition to academic libraries across the globe. Again, each library wishes to have a rich cellular of facts and communique generation and manpower to function it. The lack of these technologies is a main problem in the current library. This unavailability of the usage of digitized types of knowledge creates an opening among the library and the scholars because the newbies are by some means taking gain of e-studying thru their android and PC which creates distrust on the gratuity in their conventional library in this college. Inside the case of academics, the troubles are more difficult. Sarowardy & Halder (2019) have shown via their findings that teachers are little frequent in the use of e-assets for making their lessons and starting up academic researches as they may be one step decrease in assessment to the scholars in case of making use of e-mastering structures. Changes in countrywide coverage to attain excellent training also can be made regarded with the aid of reading inside the library due to the fact the library is a treasure trove of know-how. Larner (2004) has also remarked on the few statistics of how a trainer leader can be benefitted via this type of arranged library as, (i) getting guide from all kinds of materials with regard to the formal and non-formal problem to be counted that might help them propose books for the learners, forming catalogs of references for them, making innovative shows for class and supporting in syllabus designing in the limitations of college (i) encouraging unbiased studying, (iii) enhancing non-public mindset and accountability and (iv) providing educational sports for the expert development.

Elevating trainer Engagement in Library activities
The maximum of the schooling of life is casual. inside the area of casual education, people take benefit of others, take advantage of the media and take advantage of the library; if

he thinks from this point on, he may want to get whatever, and he should get from formal training. Kate (2010) defines teacher leader duties inside the following two diversions: (i) export obligations and (ii) Administrative duties. As consistent with their professional obligations, a pacesetter can discover what resources are wanted for his or her area, an anthropologist can educate students approximately research, referencing, and plagiarism and direct the students to trust that using the library will enhance the skills of students to work with their everyday works. Via the use of a library, a library can fine use of (i) effective use of resources, (ii) right use of teaching time, and the improvement of literacy may be performed with the aid of obtaining skills in languages, arts, mathematics, records, and many others.

Now the query comes the way to boost the engagement of the lecturers in library sports. Schlak (2017) has proposed few methods the way to boost instructor engagement in library activities. The writer proposes that ideas of institutional assist, transactional motive, collaborative and shared gaining knowledge of approach can build stimulus to the teachers to be involved in library sports. The institutional help within the case of the look at university is to elevate funds for the library. But the most important issue is to divide a proper time of library use in order that the teachers may have time sufficient apart from their instructional sports to visit the library. Transactional engagement serves the cause of enticing all participants of the group to learn and create a social bonding among most of the participants of the organization. In this situation, the improvement of trainer-student dating out of study room, then designing a program, numerous competitive activities, providing extra responsibilities to the students with the help of library will make library greater focused; with a purpose to bring the lecturers and newbies lower back to the library. This is a triangular assignment that needs to be assisted by the college authority, the teachers, and the librarian or library assistants. The cutting-edge way of studying and distribution of know-how has not been an independent project. Organization work, shared learning, disbursed understanding have were given momentum as a substitute. The library can assist in this respect as it's a place of pupil-teacher friendly engagement. The instructor should construct capability at the materialization of shared getting to know. The university authority can take steps to teach the lecturers on the character of distributed studying and how it makes an instructor leader.

The challenges identified through take a look at

The usage of various resources in the library calls for many forms of education. If these instructions are not located in the correct and easy language, the users will no longer be able to use the library well. However, the library of this have a look at the location is profuse with formal collections of books on nearly every shelf. Different fictions and non-fictions, books from the English writers, the very current nice seller books, books on records, and technology are a rarity that is the primary and predominant venture for this library.

The surroundings of this library aren't congenial. A library is an area of relaxation, social gathering, and shared learning. So, the surroundings must be of such type in order that the site visitors can experience comfort in it.

This library can accommodate the most effective much less than ten contributors and over and over there, a liberation struggle nook has been hooked up within the library via the steering of the university authority which nails down the distance of the library. Because it has been indicated earlier than that it's a government-backed university and all of the budgetary allocations are made by using the government. The university receives a little price range for the development of the library. This insufficient fund poses limitations to enhance the library in a new and current fashion with the inclusion of all essential tools and devices. Bainbridge et al. (2002) have conducted studies considering that 1999 to 2000 on one hundred and seventy respondents wherein they found that the functionality of a library relies largely on the instructor-librarian and sufficient group of workers as they can at once help the academics with designing curriculum and selecting substances for each the teachers and the students. But the remembering of regret Bainbridge et al. (2002) expressed that maximum of Canadian schools is reducing library staff from the educational institutions. This kind of problem prevails in these institutions as this organization lacks a librarian who has a degree on Library sciences. Most effective two college staffs from administrative assistants had been ordained as responsibility staffs. The contemporary country of the library on the university isn't constructive. Despite the fact that there's an assemblage of books here, that isn't sufficient. The maximum is old and unpopular books. There's no mag. there is no professional librarian. After the ultimate of college hour library additionally closes at that time. The positional issue also does not match. The range of different books out of doors the textbook is very few. No periodicals are posted. No activity is available regarding modern-day information availability. So, it is smooth know-how remember that the present-day library of the college isn't suitable to fulfill the need of rookies.

The management of the demanding situations

The first and predominant assignment is to consist of the innovative staff (they will be a teacher on demand) for the library if it is not feasible to recruit a certified librarian because of the character of this college. Then the dutiful instructor of the library needs to perceive which styles of books are to be had in the library after which ask for assist from every teacher via management which forms of books want to be accrued for the scholars in addition to for the teachers. Present-day informative books on science, generation, career-making plans, global coverage, and politics need to be covered in the library. Numerous and qualitative collections play a large position within the mastering of the student, and as an end result, various and qualitative collections ought to be adopted. There needs to be sufficient space for a look at. Scheduling the timing is to receive precedence because the engagement of the lecturers in library sports is the high situation for this take a look at, so scheduling suitable library hours declare prime concern. Then, the library must devise the approaches and policies the way to combine advanced ICT facilities within the library. After that, orientation to the library facilities, the necessity of library work need to be imparted by way of of the library and university authority in order that the lecturers and beginners can realize what the assets the library is offering and what the programs the library is devising to be able to have interaction the lecturers and the scholars in library work as Schlak (2017) have the conviction that orientation to the library capabilities will offer mental motivation to the visitors in-campus who will come to learn how their time may be correctly utilized by being engaged in the educational library. Bello (2017) shows the better degree of involvement a trainer-librarian has in the college curriculum, the better will be the level of success of students in reading competencies, vocational take a look at competencies with a much broader breadth first-rate of reading. So, instructor engagement orientated manner needs are conducted.

The curriculum isn't always entire without college students or learners. Consequently, the implementation of curriculum occurs when the student learns experience, understanding, skills, ideas, visions, desires to achieve. It's far critical to observe that the curriculum implementation and improvement procedure maintains seamlessly with the contributors - instructors, college inspectors, examiners, and teachers - librarians and other employees. Bello (2017) has shown that the library has a totally superb aspect to a professional instructor's college sports or education. Instructors who are worried about the library and library sports are extra exciting in coaching, suitable at writing, and notably; they're up to date and more gifted in teachers.

The achievement of any academic organization is viable if there is a great quality studying environment. From this point of view, the library is regarded as a medium or medium of better schooling. The library enhances the getting to know abilities of teachers and students. Moreover, the library is regarded as the principal component of educational institutions for various motives. The library acknowledges discretion in achieving holistic and specialized components of schooling. It's an important part of the educational institution. The library performs an important role in shaping educational aspects and future generations. Here students can find out and broaden their abilities and capabilities and instructors can improve their talents. This has a look attended to become aware of why an instructor uses the library for their expert development. It additionally tended to bridge that instructor-leader is an issue of acquiring information regarding the contemporary modifications in education and abilities to handle the novices. However, this school fails to address the engagement of the lecturers in library work, shared studying, and so forth. And the reason behind this has been diagnosed as the present library system inside the university that is opposite to the growing demand of library as growing an inventive, skillful instructor. The want for this college is to implement an updated library facility earlier than laboring for growing trainer-leader via non-stop expert development as the library assists in the non-stop professional improvement of an instructor.

Implementation and recommendation

The purpose of this look at the change to get the academics in continuous expert improvement so that you can increase their expertise as teacher-leader. so that you can do so, the look at diagnosed or tried to make a connection between the usage of the library and becoming instructor-leader. However, the study finds that teachers are reluctant to apply to the library in this faculty and the central purpose of the instructor's reluctance is recognized as the lack of the right schedule, surroundings, collections, and e-studying facility triumphing in this faculty library. for this reason, some important tips want to be bestowed to make the library operational for the gain of the teachers:

1. Figuring out the academics for the motive of the use of the university library.

2 To discover what's available within the library

3. Understanding the offerings of the library gives

4. Understanding how teachers use the library to improve their academic excellence

5. Organizing relationships between library use and instructors' gaining knowledge of activities

6. Enhancing and helping the desires contained inside the university Curriculum

7. Use of facts in technology, imagination, knowledge, and intake - providing opportunities to enjoy

8. Offering gets admission to nearby, state, national, and worldwide sources so that students can reproduce anti thoughts and critiques.

9. Organizing sports to encourage cultural and social recognition for instructors

10. Working collectively with pals, parents, teachers, administrators to gain the dreams of the university.

Chapter Four

Social Interaction among Teachers and Students

Training is a procedure that allows mastering while supplying knowledge and competencies that is transferred from humans to humans. Getting to know is accomplished through exclusive mediums such as research and discussion. Dictionary.com defined schooling as a technique wherein humans transfer expertise and statistics, (dictionary.com). in step with the sector bank's view as it relates to schooling, it's far stated that schooling plays a crucial position in poverty discount, enhancing one's general of dwelling and developing stability. it is each a guided process and a character's self-educating commitment. Based on one's society and culture, the younger persons are usually trained via those who are older. Due to man or woman's understanding, the know-how of subjects and topics and life stories, he/she is taken into consideration well-educated and academically wealthy. The social mastering approach grounds itself within the perception that human behavior is determined by using the relationship among cognitive elements, environmental effects, and conduct. It proposes that new behaviors may be received by means of watching and imitating others. Constructivism is of the view that novices include a spread of expertise, feelings, and capabilities and that that is where gaining knowledge must begin. it's miles based totally on the perception that scholars construct their own information and understanding. In my coaching, those aspects both play a quintessential role in the studying environment. For the functions of this mission, I'm able to attend on the social getting to know approach.

In order for mastering to be performed, there are instructional instructions that need to be observed, in order that people can recognize, assess, significantly and efficiently examine, compare, make knowledgeable selections and judgment which could be very important to one's development. The training procedure includes years of attending faculty that stages from preschool to college even as incorporating many subjects or even cultures. Also, for studying to be found out, each trainer must teach easily and with clarity. Both students and teachers ought to be clean with the subjects discussed in any other case confusion inside the thoughts can be developed and the gaining knowledge of outcome can be a terrible one. In a few societies, studying isn't finished due to the unavailability of training as a result of a variety of limitations. However, every man or woman ought to have the same opportunity to schooling without being discriminated against. The manner in which a trainer presents students with a subject remember could be very essential in the direction of their gaining knowledge; instructors should be nicely organized and should interact with each student. Additionally, they need to boost behaviors by using the usage of various strategies which might be available. It's far expected that teachers might be dedicated, focused, and inclined to work with the scholars and impart know-how unto them. It's far crucial that both the teachers and the students succeed at the goals that they had set forth. Many faculties are bothered institutions that have been struggling with pupil's engagement and evaluation effects. That allows you to remedy the taking place situation, the faculties have employed a set of tutorial consultants to deal with those issues. These specialists will do study room observations, accumulate facts, and analyze their findings. Through this, treasured remarks might be furnished to the teachers and faculty administrators so as to enhance mastering. We have finished our observations and we will present a report with our guidelines. These methods are primarily based on our revel in as educators and our expertise in studying theory.

Some have determined a grade-five bodily training elegance. The teacher's technique is behavioral. He shapes conduct through rewards (compliments) and punishments. This was also very clear to look at with his control fashion. The notion of the entire lesson become very teacher-led and there has been now not sufficient to indicate that he turned into concerned with the students' knowledge of the content material. This particular lesson centered on the psychomotor domain. Under is a report with my observations and suggestions. The teacher got here three minutes past due. By means of this time, some college students were going for walks approximately, some had been seated having a talk or scrolling their phones. The teacher needs to have been available before the students and had the health club geared up for the deliberate sports. This sets the tone for the lesson. If the teacher who is supposed to model true practice cannot be stricken to be on time then this could negatively impact the students.

The instructor then referred to the scholars and addressed them. He informed them that they were going to have a basketball lesson. First, they have been to perform little drills after which end off with a basketball sport. The trainer proved about five one-of-a-kind drills, highlighting the key points they needed to look out for. As they discovered the scholars, a few were attentive and listening while the others had been really no longer engaged. The scholars had been then led by way of the teacher via a heat up recurring which lasted about five minutes. This a part of the lesson might have been extra enticing. According to Gagne, the instructor could have attempted to gain students' attention by providing an interest that might stimulate the students with novelty, uncertainty, and marvel. The intention ought to additionally have been really communicated, the students made privy to the evaluation approaches and what success might appear like. they might additionally advocate that the instructor guides the scholars to mirror their modern or prior information of the aim and why it is crucial to research. Intention placing, remarks, and reflection is crucial for effective gaining knowledge. "Social cognitive principle contends that dreams beautify mastering and performance thru their outcomes on perceptions of development, self-efficacy, and self-evaluations". The instructor modeling the drills became a good concept due to the fact "we soak up more data visually than in another sense." but, there were many drills for the students to don't forget and ought to have damaged them down separately. Higher nonetheless, he may want to have involved his college students as fashions, sought their perspectives, and looked for expertise. The students then went into the drills for the following 20 minutes with occasional water breaks. All through this time, he gave positive remarks and encouragement and additionally punished those who regarded no longer to be doing the drills proper or messing about with a fixed of push-united states of America or laps around the health club. I observed that a few college students struggled to execute the activities and others did no longer take the exercise critically and appeared unmotivated to examine.

Looking at this part, they questioned if any of the scholars knew why they had been doing the drills they have been doing apart from the unison solution of "getting better". They had endorse using the learner targeted technique whilst planning. Questions like: who're these college students and what are their hobbies? How does the mastering goal connect to them? What motivates them? For the scholars who were struggling to execute the drills. They might endorse that the teacher should differentiate the instructions based on the readiness or ability of the students. Rather he punished them with strolling laps. "Learner-centered instructors present college students with "simply possible difficulties" that is, tough sufficient to hold engagement, however now not as hard as to lead to discouragement. The instructor ought to be extra considerate with reference to what the studying purpose for the lesson is and how the scholars will explore their knowledge. For instance, he would have had much less complicated drills for the novices. "Having high expectations of our college students does not mean that we have the identical expectancies". They would also recommend that scholars work in small agencies to create their very own drills to help them enhance unique skills that have been tested by way of the trainer. They might in addition make bigger this through developing (with steerage) their personal small-sided games to peer the application/ relevance of the abilities they're being taught. This will be a thoughtful method that would interact with the students extra. Jensen (1998) describes the significance of students operating collectively and the value of collaboration for the effective improvement of wondering methods. The scholars had a spoil in which the instructor counseled them on their efforts, explained the policies of the subsequent (a recreation of basketball), and sorted them into two groups. The kids performed and he changed into the referee. On the top of the sport, the scholars were given their luggage and left the gymnasium headed to their next class. Once more, the students had been being talked to, and that the instructor did no longer appear to test for expertise. I notion some demonstrations regarding the policies would have worked nicely more so if modeled via one of the college students. They had ideas in the course of the game, brief and sharp remarks would have been useful. However, additionally, peer evaluation right from the drilling stage and via the whole lesson. There was no conclusion at the end of the lesson. This could have been an extremely good possibility for the students to mirror what they have learned, for both the instructor and college students to test for the expertise and likely suggest methods of having better. Basic, the teacher is teaching in a conventional style that is outdated. The student engagement at the cognitive and affective area infrequently existent but there is room to increase all domain names. This variety enables the creation of more properly-rounded learning reports and meets a number of studying patterns and studying modalities and students create extra neural networks and pathways for that reason helping consider. The instructor seems to be the handiest source of information and often talks to the students hardly creating possibilities for them to express their perspectives and to examine each other.

Report one

They determined a grade three Social research teacher; the instructor and the scholars were early for class. The topic for dialogue changed into tradition. The instructor had requested each student in a previous elegance to return to magnificence with a cultural item for dialogue. The items that were offered blanketed food, tack, and apparel, and as the scholars provided, each object became discussed and the students made contributions. The instructor then positioned the students into businesses and allowed them to be creative by means of giving displays on extraordinary cultures. The students had masses of amusing as they sing, acted, and danced. The lesson became nicely carried out and the instructor became glad about the interaction of the specific cultures coming collectively to create studying possibilities.

Report two

A file on Sunnydale School: The challenges and suggestions. The Sunnydale school is situated in city place, that covers the part of town and village effect, and the analysis of the personal reviews documented in the records book of the faculty management preserved to the college manager well-known shows that sixty percentage inexperienced persons represent the village-based center or lower-middle-class own family while the relaxation forty percent novices constitute metropolis primarily based higher magnificence circle of relatives. So, the novices here are determined to reveal combined tendency and aptitude and community know-how as well as facilitation delivered from their network. This is the overall situation of the learners who decide that they've various tastes, expertise, and mindset. Again, the teachers are from very average capabilities heritage having little specialized schooling on training and student psychology. Those issues get up as predominant challenges after studying the statistics retrieved from the investigation.

Commentary of instructors

As experts, this group visited some faculties to study instructors at distinctive tiers and at extraordinary places to recognize there, control competencies, techniques of teaching, and their interplay with students. Throughout the observations, we noticed that some of the lecturers attended class overdue even as others had been early and thoroughly prepared. We additionally noticed that in the faculties wherein instructors have been past due, the students tend to be very unsettled in place of the colleges where teachers have been punctual and very prepared. The scholars there were eager and excited to take on their duties; they were also very interactive with every difference in spite of their specific cultures and backgrounds. What was also discovered was that a few instructors confirmed challenges in the direction of the scholars' gaining knowledge of and there was overall cooperation between teachers and college students. Some of the lecturers placed the scholars into companies for special sports so that they can proportion their unique thoughts and opinions. Another commentary coming from a document from certainly one of the faculties in the urban area states that the greater percent of the college's population is from lower-class families. Additionally, instructors at the school are not exposed to specialized training.

Interview of the learner

The faculties provide lab facilities, statistics, and conversation-based total classroom, computer, and projector centers in most of the lessons. but, the interview of five of the scholars selected purposively presents the data that (a) teachers rely on a lecture to behavior lessons, (b) instructors make one presentation on average per week, © the teachers cannot show gifted in running multimedia in the study room. Penuel et al. (2000) contend the credibility of the usage of multimedia in coaching as it gives much scope to the freshmen to "prepare, synthesize and increase" an eye-catching reveal in of visible contents that they learned audibly. This statement made by way of Penuel et al. validates the inevitability of using multimedia in the schoolroom and that is why; the schooling area has moved to comprise multimedia in the teaching/learning process. However, the interview reviews on the scholars of the colleges gift the reality that it's far one of the demanding situations of this faculty.

A survey on the lecturers

A questionnaire survey changed into performed on the ten instructors from one of the colleges in which we attempted to degree the expert competencies and their perspectives on the negative consequences of students to make a comparison between the perspectives of instructors and college students. The seven teachers did not have any commencement degree on MEd even though all have got schooling on pedagogy for a month or forty-five days. However, no one agrees that the digital content material-based totally coaching method is the answer to learner's poor success. All of the contributors agreed on the issue that the network difference hampers learners' standard achievement. The commentary from the survey file is that teachers accept as true with that it's miles the social, cultural and family background that influence the getting to know of the scholars and as the students of the school hail from the village both urban and city; they show numerous aptitude and tendency to mastering. but the latest have a look at on the variations of college students' community and surety of identical talent shows that a design is required to make certain community-based surroundings within the classroom that Schunk (2012) highlighted inside the bankruptcy six within the 'learning Theories: an academic angle'. John Dewey (1916) also notes that a child ought to be ensured that it is able to observe its community expertise inside the magnificence and study room know-how in its community. Thus, it's miles quite a mistake to deduce that the terrible performance of the beginners may be investigated in the light of network variations that the academics agreed without dispute.

The evaluations of lesson plans

Our cognizance had been also on the observation and analysis of lesson plans of some classes as direct class commentary may additionally restrict an instructor's herbal conduct in a category that could impact negatively on my findings. After reviewing five lesson plans from five teachers we located that the lecturers depend on lecture methods in disseminating statistics. They have very little software for the workout of three domains (cognitive, affective, and psychomotor domains) in the lecture room. The lesson plans maintain little or no possibility of QA consultation on the end of the elegance. Accordingly, the lesson plans provide the concept that the lecturers come what may neglect the scholar/teacher interaction and inexperienced persons participatory approach in the study room.

After reviewing the lesson plans, interviewing the learners, and accomplishing a survey on teachers, some issues had been recognized and we trust that these problems are growing barriers to the freshmen to analyze and make a permanent impact on their learned knowledge. So, we endorsed that:

1.   The school authority has to encourage the academics to finish a grasp's degree on training for a sound understanding of pedagogy.

2.   The lecturers should increase competencies to apply multimedia in training to provide content material greater enjoyably as learners analyze via entertainment.

3.   The authority should set up a workshop for the fast foundation on forming lesson plans.

 Inexperienced persons have to be deemed as important to instructors, and in spite of the challenges of an organization to fulfill up the needs of beginners who constitute multifarious network studies, and it ought to be clearly stated that the lecturers have essential roles to play within the stage of training that the scholars receive and the method in which it's far performed. but, many of them have located to have little understanding inside the fields of training, current findings, and improvements applied in schooling. It's far essential that instructors receive periodical training on problems and situations that create boundaries to effective teaching and mastering.

Bodily education Basketball lesson plan

Lesson objective:

•   College students explore the extraordinary approaches to dribble the ball on the spot and at the flow: At varying heights, the use of specific palms, and in the three planes of motion.

•   College students to research conditions in which every one of these explorations might be efficient alternatives to manipulate the ball if confronted with an opponent.

Device

•   A basketball according to pupil

•   A playing region with a difficult floor with line-markings at different distances

•   A whistle

•   A whiteboard

•   10 squares marked out

Lesson introduction

• inform students of the lesson consciousness for the day (dribbling)

• Ask students to percentage their reports of dribbling. What's it? Why is it useful in basketball? Are there efficient ways of dribbling towards an opponent/ without an opponent?

• Standard dynamic heat up with a ramification of actions accompanied via dynamic stretches.

 essential a part of the lesson

• Every pupil requested to dribble the ball around the corridor for two minutes.

• College students are then prompted by using the trainer to dribble: instantaneous, at the move, at varying heights/speeds/route or planes, and by way of changing the dribbling palms

• proportion their experiences of the pastime beneath teacher steerage. What was smooth? What became tough? Cautioned approaches of getting better?

• Teacher demonstration of dribbling movements that might be taken into consideration efficiently, highlighting teaching factors and directing the students to the displayed suggestions on the whiteboard.

• Students repeat above interest – now mindful of the teaching points.

• Finally, students pair up. One of them with a ball even as both of them are inner a 10-meter rectangular marked out via cones. The student without the ball tries to dispose of the only with it. If successful, the roles change. (three to five-minute pastime)

• The scholar pairs reflect by means of sharing stories of

the lesson, that specialize in their successes and challenges. We then make connections of the dribbling pastime to the actual recreation and proportion techniques for getting higher. What type of mindset do we want to get better? (Self-Efficacy).

Improvements

Using the social cognitive approach, I have to have a clearer and unique goal for my college students at the beginning of the lesson. These are the dreams that might power learning for my college students. Schunk (2012) notes that "Social cognitive theory contends that goals decorate learning and overall performance through their outcomes on perceptions of progress, self-efficacy, and self-opinions".

This may also improve the instructor modeling part of the lesson via providing a spread of models from the magnificence (students) to illustrate the dribbling actions. They hired cognitive modeling in my lesson instance, however, they could observe it up with extra factors of self-coaching like overt guidance wherein the kids carry out the dribble beneath my route and progressively develop it to via these steps. "Overt self-steerage: child plays while self-instructing aloud. Dwindled overt self-steering: baby whispers instructions even as appearing mission. Covert self-education: infant plays even as guided by way of inner silent speech."

They might additionally take into account displaying videos of hit dribblers, executing the movement, and talking approximately how they attained that level of proficiency. Models who've won distinction are more apt to command attention than those of decrease prestige. They had additionally needed a terrific kind of fashions, bearing in mind that elements including gender and age can have a profound effect on mastering. Terrible stereotyping wields a lingering impact on folks who revel in it, even as UNESCO list pupils with "special academic wishes or disabilities, ladies, and learner from minority groups", as individuals who are maximum at threat from stereotyping.

In phrases of evaluation, they could improve this by means of incorporating the idea of recording the scholars performing the motion after which using the self-modeling strategy. I might manual them thru the analysis in their movement as vital. Schunk mentioned that "Self-modeling kids scored better on self-efficacy for getting to know, motivation, and posttest self-efficacy and achievement."

In conclusion, I trust that the social and constructivist theories have commonalities and that they are able to both aid students' gaining knowledge in significant ways. Getting a deeper understanding of the social cognitive principle has truly made me keep in mind the usage of models inside the studying journey of my college students.

Morality behavior

Because it relates to social interplay, morality behaviors can in no way be dissuaded from working towards in every respect of lifestyles as Schon feld et al has posited the concept that morality is the ecliptic and the first 'solar ladder' (to transport human lifestyles in a pure and sophisticated way). This natural and complex manner of human questioning and behavior is massive for a society that will enlarge to a greater nation. Those authors are having speculated on the necessity of Ethics and values for the sustainable development of a state. And students are to be the torchbearers of sustainable developments for a state as today's youngsters are the following day's country-wide builder in this and those ways. Highlighting the need of the kids to construct a country, Mikhail has cited a citation by former secretary widespread of UN Baan ki Moon in which the author has quoted "let us renowned and rejoice what children can do to build a more secure, more just global". This reference fosters the concept that the kids ought to construct (i) a more secure and (ii) a simple world. And a teen learns what's just if they're moral in thinking and ethical in behavior. This fosters that the exercising of morality behavior by the various students (who can be addressed as children) is vital. A learner is inspired with own family, surroundings, and educational establishments wherein they study each behavior suitable for the concord, peace, and properly-being of the society. inline with Frederick Froebel, 'kids are the garden plant life. The teacher is his gardener. The assignment of the instructor is to cautiously increase the seedlings. it is the duty of the instructor to broaden honesty and social features which can be hidden in the toddler ' Referenced from Joyce and Weil. Teachers have been characterized as catalysts of behavior molding the various learners which applies that instructors play roles significantly at the getting to know and enhancing of morality behaviors among the newcomers. One of the brilliant hobbies of information distribution is teaching. All through a while, instructors have performed a position within the formation of societies with human and ethical values. Confucius, the historical spiritual chief of China, says, "Teachers may be the supply of know-how and awareness. He can be an excellent ruler " Cartwright.

Now the question of 'what is moral behavior?' is applicable to specify with a view to identifying which the student morality behavior is. Gert and Gert have designated morality conduct as the rational, correct conduct that's socially established and the intention of this socially prevalent behavior is concord and peace in the society. Thus, Weissbourd has marked on the troubles of (i) the moral conduct of college students, and (ii) the responsibility of the teachers to teach ethical behaviors to the students. The writer has said that the public holds the notion at the fact that educational institutions ought to ameliorate greed, delinquency and disregard widely widespread a few college students. Accordingly, the author has tried to signify pupil moral conduct but no longer proscribing most effective on these items. The purpose of student moral behavior gaining knowledge of is to be a complete individual with moral, ethical, emotional, and rational aptitude.

This r is evolved on three key principles, consisting of; (i) the idea of scholar morality conduct, (iii) the way of development of the scholar morality conduct, and (iii) the concern of such development in the colleges of Bangladesh. This paper tries to evaluate the scope and opportunity of coaching and studying morality behaviors in the faculties of Bangladesh. This paper tends to sort out the manner how instructional establishments can thrive to make certain morality behavior exercising in elegance rooms handiest if the remedial step is required. the faculties of Bangladesh appeared because the regions of case research because the latest upward push of intolerance, scandals, killings of fellow pals many of the students of university ranges of Bangladesh are apparent. Kamol, a reporter of English day by day, interviewed one among reputed college vice-chancellors where the vice-chancellor retorted, "Regrettably, fellow feeling and respect for fellow students are regularly lacking these days. Frequently loss of recognition for the teachers is found, which not a great sign is in any given society." This triumphing situation fosters the concept that the schools of Bangladesh cannot cope with the need for moral behavior and make a manner out to nourish those in educational institutions. This prevailing gap made to search for a solution of the speculation that 'the faculties of Bangladesh loss of teaching and improving morality behaviors the various college students of Bangladesh'.

Kamol has additionally reported that the alphabet teaching in the beyond began with ethical teachings which the texts of contemporary time are lacking. The unfolding of technology and technology, contemporary communique devices, the internet, and mobile connectivity have made the educational content paradigm shift. So, the academic device, institutions, and teachers have more roles to make the beginners on target as the function of the instructor may be very vital and effective in developing ethical values for a number of the students. In any scholar's existence, the role of the teacher is very a good deal encouraged with the aid of the family or the figure. Instructors are the sense of right and wrong of the US, and the outstanding craftsman of the enlightened country and human assets. Whilst a human toddler reaches the age of school or now and again even before, she or he comes in contact with the trainer at any degree at some stage in the complete lifestyles and it'll have an everlasting effect in their lifestyles. In keeping with Ryan ok in his quick history of ethical schooling, Maximum thinkers, instructional practitioners, and mother and father acknowledge that youngsters are born helpless and want the care and steering of adults into their teens and frequently pass.

The development of training is to be measured with outside and interior improvement of a scholar which the educational machine of Bangladesh is lacking at the back of. The scholars are being brought up with excessive performances in sciences and technologies as well as an ethical and moral impairment which disrupt the true reason of schooling Kamol. However, the take a look at tends to focus on the role of the academics in this era to make the students morally dwelling alongside the instructional performance as academic performance isn't the simplest achievement of medals but also improvement of moral behaviors.

The time period 'Morality conduct' is an embedded phrase of (i) moralization and (ii) behavior. The behavior which has been moralized may be termed as 'Morality behavior'. Behavior is any kind of movement and the preceding of morality before behavior specifies the kind and approaches of behavior. Consequently, the morality behavior desires to be clarified with the help of literature where the researchers in addition to thinkers have tried how to outline morality and conduct.

The term 'Morality' is an abstract one via its very own nature. Moreover, this term has been considered and reviewed by way of the philosophers, psychologists, thinkers from their views. Gert and Gert have defined 'Morality' on the idea of points of view, that is; (i) descriptive and (ii) normative. The descriptive point of view describes morality as a code of conduct, or accurate behaviors, set by way of the religions or society which the community people ought to comply with so one can live in that society with symmetry. However, the second factor of view, on the whole, relies upon the character choice. The action which appears rational to the person gets abode in their mind and that they practice these of their normal life terming them as ethical practices. for this reason, morality receives a specification relying on the man or woman selections which emerge thru the rationality that every person possesses.

Right here, Gert and Gert have clarified the fact that character cognition assists people in adopting moral behavior. However, this ideation creates a vacuum as to who's the one's individuals that follow or can apply cognition to decide which is moral. Furthermore, the exercise of each person's morality creates disharmony in a society that can cause crumbling of society, at the least a network. This initiative the concept of agreeing on the descriptive point of view because the moral behavior must possess a normal, or countrywide, or a social, or community code which the human beings throughout that circle follow.

It is now applicable quarry who determines the code of moral behavior. Brent & Evelyn states that it's far very difficult to country the determinants of code of moral conduct in this period of multiculturalism. they have got initiated a query concerning the problem of the Jew cleansing as Jew were a part of the German morality code of conducts earlier than WW II, however, why they have been subjugated to concentration camps is the query that shakes the appropriateness of the code of morality conduct set by means of the society. However, they have the consent on few main assets of determining morality. They agree on (i) 'Cultural Relativism' and (ii) 'Divine Command concept' along with (iii) 'ethical Subjectivism' and (iv) 'ethical Egoism'. Social in addition to spiritual institutions come to the fore if the sources of institutionalization are considered.

Training is a lifelong technique. Extra in particular for the priority of the ambitions and scope of this paper, the schooling that is institutionalized by means of colleges, colleges, and universities is being taken into consideration for the assessment. Little has evaluated such kind of institutional training as it's miles a system of socialization by using teaching inexperienced persons with 'cultural expectancies and norms'. The lecturers, textbooks in addition to classmates enhance those right into a learner. Morality behavior is one of the cultural expectancies and norms. Therefore, educational institutions have turned to be an entity of instructing moral behavior. Now at the forefront of the twenty-first century, a qualifying time period has been added earlier than education and it sounds like first-class education. United Nations has for the first time addressed schooling with such emphasis that the concept of 'nice training' has been set as SDG-4 (Sustainable development goal) some of the seventeen goals which are about to be met with the aid of the member nations via 2030. (i) Inclusiveness, (ii) equitability, and (iii) durability all through life had been made because of the defining characteristics of fine training. Slade has referred that satisfactory education includes a baby's intellectual, emotional, moral, bodily, and cognitive development in order that it turns into a lively citizen of the nation who will uphold peace, concord, and prosperity to their society. but, the 21st-century training or exceptional education, how we explain the time period, cannot cease from the way of teaching morality to nourish ethical and disciplined conduct most of the beginners.

Bidwell establishes the idea in his paper that values and moral behaviors may be found out via right socialization as socialization is the sum total of values and ethical behaviors which might be representational in the context of network or society. The instructional institution is one of the finest industries that foster the socialization of a member little. For this reason, ethical grounding, socialization, and educational institutions are interlinked as well as intra-connected with each other. Accordingly, the role of an educational institution in the technique of socialization via imparting moral behavior to beginners can never be constrained.

Pels and Ruyter have labored on the radicalization of teenagers and determined training, as well as socialization, has an incredible effect on radicalization and that they have contended that the moral and religious values of the dad and mom and teachers help teenagers inculcate that ideology imposed on them. Right here, the inculcation of ethical and moral ideals has been shown depending notably on the teachers aside from their dad and mom. And a teacher exposes any form of ideology to the scholars in the instructions with the assist of textbooks. Therefore, the magnificence lectures of a trainer in addition to the messages of textbooks exposed by using the lecturers to the students turn out to be the best media for a teacher which helps them guide the beginners. Here, the willingness of the academics or the competence of them, as well as the valuable textbooks as sources to examine ethical behavior, are emergent.

The previous literature has strived to make clear the concept of morality, ethical behavior, the position of the educational institutions and instructors so as to inculcate moral conduct in the freshmen. And the literature has also made connections to the manner of institutional socialization with most of these behavioral moldings. It fosters the concept that institutions pave the way to socialization and the newbies examine the moral codes of conducts well-known in the society through this manner. But the academic institutions have also pragmatic points of view on the necessity for growing human assets amid the challenges of the globalized competitions posited thru information and generation. From this factor of view, the need and worth of an institution based on the instructional performances on the part of the beginners are to be granted as big. It exposes the reality of an academic institution as an author of educational performers. Now, the point of debate is whether the teaching of moral conduct and academic performance align, whether or not faculties dissuade the route of morality behavior coaching that allows you to emphasize handiest on the academic performance.

Academic overall performance has two dimensions, (i) person instructional performance and (i) cumulative academic overall performance. Character educational overall performance is based totally on the efforts of the inexperienced persons and their familial help. But cumulative academic performance is predicated on the efforts of the institutions. Kassarnig et al have studied the problems of educational performances and located that socialization of the novices helps to grow instructional performances. The learners who're more energetic in the socialization manner initiated by using the academic institutions have been capable to expose pleasant educational performances as those novices have already followed shared getting to know and are corresponding to organization work, disbursed research. This study has advocated that the way of raising educational overall performance most of the newcomers are to involve the rookies in extra socialization procedure as this manner facilitates to elevate instructional performances.

Therefore, the idea of coaching morality behavior in addition to that of elevating instructional overall performance fosters the urgency of the socialization system from the part of the educational establishments. The institutions have each opportunity to impact undoubtedly at the problems of educational performance and morality conduct. Morality conduct teaching is not possible without proper socialization and proper socialization results in better instructional performances. And this kind of is embedded with the phrases of first-rate training rather emphasized through the 'aim- four of Sustainable development desires 'proposed by means of the united countries that's to be met via 2030.

However, some of these promising notes fail if the state of affairs of the morality conduct teaching, getting to know and training are considered inside the context of the education of Bangladesh. Ray has studied these troubles at the University of Dhaka and pronounced the educational gadget of Bangladesh necessarily fails to deal with the morality schooling at the side of diverse preferred and technical. Furthermore, the paper reveals that ninety eight% replied felt dissatisfaction even as reporting to the supply of morality schooling and morality exercise in the campus or classrooms, and 95% of respondents agreed with the truth that the present curriculum has faults that cannot deal with the necessity of ethical education. It's far their opinion to revise the curriculum straight away as they file that extortion, delinquency, teasing, and disregard are harnessing unexpectedly due to the lack of ethical training. This supplied the fodder for the researcher to find out whether or not the freshmen within the college level of Bangladesh feel the same and whether they're well socialized through academic institutions apart from the simplest textual provisions.

The few principal questions developed the floor of this

book as to (i) the scope of gaining knowledge of morality within the school room context, (ii) the reaction of the scholars regarding the availability of studying and exercise of morality inside the magnificence room and (iii) the manner out of checking scholar morality deterioration through institutionalization. on the way to look at at the stated issues, the researcher meant to degree the frequency of the supply/unavailability of studying-exercise of morality in schoolroom context, and fostered description of the findings. in keeping with Bernard, the Qualitative method describes "a situation, phenomenon, trouble or event" on a nominal scale method. This Book studies the prevailing situation at the lessons of morality within the lecture rooms and it tries to analyze whether or not the inexperienced persons are glad about the preparations from the part of the establishments in order that the novices can work out morality in institutions. once more, a few close-ended questions helped to gather the information that aimed to quantify the frequencies of responses at the issues of (i) institutional provisions of morality classes, (ii) the scope of college students to exercise morality in establishments like "sure, no, glad, disillusioned, and many others." this information will help to quantify what number of teachers sense satisfied or unsatisfied with the overall arrangements of multimedia in that university. Those styles of data present the number of responses. for this reason, the paper consists of a triangulation of multiple approaches, this is; qualitative and quantitative strategies for the reason to perceive the number of the respondents aggrieved as well as to realize the conception of moral conduct that the respondents feel to be and to do. Teddlie and Tashakkori have proposed that the triangulation of strategies is a positivist outlook within the fields of research and it's frequently looked for method as it enables to analyze each numeric and descriptive facts a good way to keep validity and reliability of the studies.

The winning kingdom of Morality Behaviour

The first actual five questions within the supplied questionnaire to the study populace aimed to delve out the extent of socialization inside the context of both family and colleges. Socialization is a manner that begins from family and matures in the academic institutions which have been elaborated at some point in the evaluations of literature. However, twenty-four(48%) individuals out of fifty spoke back that they do no longer choose to remain in touch with relatives on an ordinary basis which presents a sort of indifference popular in the novices concerning the essence of familial bonding. again, the considerable number of respondents had an opinion at the truth that the academic establishments of Bangladesh cannot provide morality teachings as 32% of respondents had responded negatively and more than 12% respondents had doubt on the possibility of morality teachings inside the classrooms although ninety six% respondents believed on the need of morality behavior practices within the academic institutions.

The extent of Institutional Provisions of Morality exercise

The following three questions were set to find out (i) whether or not the respondents were glad at the moral behavior of the scholars, (ii) whether or not the respondents had been happy at the provisions of moral teachings designed by means of the curriculum and (iii) whether the respondents were happy at the availability of practice of moral behavior in the classroom situations. let the triad sides of dissatisfaction ratio be proven through wherein the 42 % respondent spoke back dissatisfaction at the student morality conduct, 40 % replied upset on the provision of morality in the curriculum. however, the very disillusioned element become the unavailability of institutional provisions where the students can't be furnished through the teachers or college administrations with the scope of practicing of morality behaviors inside the classroom and out of the classroom staying in campus.

The elements associated with the reasons of moral Deterioration

The final questions had been set as open-ended questions. These questions sought to find out the cause of moral degradation and the manner to checking the moral degradation of some of the students. The fifty respondents drew attention to thirteen factors accountable for the moral degradation of the various college students.

A qualitative query was conducted to get the motive of student ethical degradation. here each participant became unbiased to supply the solution and no clue/hints turned into preset Four college students expressed the view that morality is deteriorating because of loss of own family education. 5% of the full students suppose that lack of circle of relatives cognizance results in degradation of morals. Seven college students consider the cheating company to be the purpose of moral turpitude. 5% of students think that morality has been missing because of the loss of religious know-how. 72% of students attributed the misuse of mobile phones and information generation to degrading morality. Three students do not forget social chaos as a reason for ethical turpitude. The remaining five college students blamed using alcohol as the main motive for the degradation of morality.

The factors related to checking moral degradation

The very last questions tried to delve out the ways of checking moral degradation because the paper tended to return to a decision of finding out a likely manner of improving morality conduct among the college students in a lecture room context with the intention to result in those practices out of the campuses and even all through their lives. The fifty college students indicated their responses in various ways which have been classified as (i) circle of relatives' responsibility, (iii) scholar self-commitment to the society, and (iv) educational institutions. Most effective four% respondents opined different methods to improve morality behaviors a number of the college students.

Whether or not the institutions advance to educate morality behaviors is beyond questions. The literature and the present findings propose that the scholars want the establishments could accord this availability in order that the newbies can get scope sufficient practice morality behaviors in the schoolroom, inside the campus. The findings propose that some forty percent of respondents trust that the instructional establishments have masses to do so as to improve the morality behavior of the students which has also been stated by means of Little.

However, the findings have additionally provided with the reality that seventy 2% of respondents trust the instructional institutions of Bangladesh (especially the institutions offering college level of training) can't arrange any form of exercise which may also assist to enhance the moral conduct of the scholars. Ray has also discovered the same information on the dearth of the negligence of the academic establishments to make a way for practicing morality conduct and this writer stated that' institutions are being influenced to serve the economic thing of the society in addition to the globe'. But why the institutions are failing has its purpose determined via the have a look at. 40% of respondents said that the curriculum of Bangladesh is defective in recognize the arrangement of moral teaching. Instructors, as well as the instructional establishments, are much more likely to follow the curriculum in preference to revising the curriculum. A maximum of the faculties of Bangladesh complies with the curriculum designed through the country-wide authority which may additionally create hollowness.

The deep evaluation shows that the individuals who had been requested to reply to the precise qualitative question "Write a cause for the scholars' ethical degradation" spoke back verities varieties of solutions. Some of the fifty respondents, 12% drew attention to the "social Chaos" even as 10% replied that the social system turned into the primary issue for moral degradation. Other college students commented on any other seven dealers being the motives for scholar morality degradation. Those have been: loss of values, disobedience to parents, the impact of overseas lifestyle, the effect of the circle of relatives' feud, misuse of records generation, misuse of cellular cellphone and drug addiction. Loss of own family education, loss of own family recognition, cheating corporation and lack of religious information have been replied as causes of student morality behavior. From this evaluation, one thing is incredible that social sickness performs a high-quality role in moral degradation. Disrespect to parents shows the looseness of own family bondage, chaos frequent in society and social machine (that provokes and conjures up delinquency) is indicated as the pivotal causes of student morality degradation. More than one circle of relatives constitutes society and various academic, social, and political establishments inclusive in this society. Consequently, the ethical degradation points to the shortage of right socialization many of the people developing up within the society. In keeping with Little instructional organization is one of the best institutions of society after own family. If the social disease is said to be responsible for pupil ethical degradation, the academic establishments need to be speculative on the issues of such types of pupil degradation.

The findings also advocate that 32% of respondents believe that instructional establishments can assist enhance the conditions and 36% of respondents depended on the need for a circle of relatives on this rely. A baby gets socialized through those two social establishments. It fosters the concept that a circle of relatives and academic establishments are conscious to dig out the reason and answer of scholar ethical degradation.

Simply, teachers construct college students into real human beings. Social, way of life, norms also have an effect on creating college students' values. The values can be created a number of the scholar via the manner of socialization. The findings mission time and time once more that the respondents were reluctant to maintain everyday contacts with the family and a number of the respondents supplied that integrity with the internet, social media, and cellular telephones are few of the causes of ethical degradation. A group can cognizance of the issue of raising social connectivity among college students. Consequently, socialization applications need to be prepared frequently in all tiers of training from primary to college. This will create a strong basis for students to have a feel of social responsibility and cultural values. As an end result, they may avoid being misled. At the identical time, they'll expand mindfulness. The developments of college students' ethical and human qualities are based totally on the triangular courting of student, instructor, and figure.

The development of human traits isn't a lot via textbooks. In this example, the encircling scenario plays a first-rate role. Students study moral and human qualities from their surroundings which fosters the concept of social integrity and interaction with a number of newbies. Similar to the development of the ethical training acquired by means of the scholars in schooling, social schooling, and human traits are learned. College students of different families have the possibility to combine with college students in training. Through this interaction, college students study and apprehend many things. Therefore, a healthy environment ought to be ensured in the instructional establishments. In lots of instances, children won't be listening to their dad and mom approximately something. Therefore, a good way to increase the ethical, social, and human features of the students, they need to first have them inside the teachers. After dad and mom, youngsters keep in mind instructors the way of existence. Despite the fact that the academic gadget is within a boundary, the students get the greatest training in lifestyles as instructors try to teach and educate college students about lifestyles. Proper coaching of the teacher performs a function in making the students as humans with human traits

Time control for instructors and students for better interplay

Time may be very essential and need to be carefully controlled. Many humans find it hard to manage their time properly; whether they may be looking to juggle work and academic responsibilities along with just getting to lessons, trying to hold up with the continuous needs of every magnificence like analyzing, or with trying to finish more than one assignments that have to be completed before the cut-off date or simply attempting to finish many obligations within their daily twenty-four (24 hrs). It is able to be laborious. Especially, in college, there are so many distractions: specific golf equipment, sports activities, and different campus activities that you could take part in, whilst seeking to collect the right grades. Time control refers to the improvement of approaches and tools that are required for efficiency and productivity. Whilst we consider time management, we have a tendency to assume personal time management, loosely defined as handling our time to waste much less time on doing the things we must do so we've got extra time to do the matters that we need to do. Consequently, time management is often the notion of or presented as a hard and fast of time. It's far the control and cognizance of a person's moves for the reason of enhancing efficiency. Its strategies contain putting attainable and workable goals, setting up priorities, skillfully utilizing the quantity of time allocated to specific obligations, and planning and scheduling the stairs needed to achieve goals. It is, therefore, advocated to plan one's work and work one's plan. When humans fail to devise, it is able to result in numerous fructuous conferences, bad conversation, and disorganized work. Time management is frequently idea of whilst we're describing assignment related to business management or government positions and attending colleges, and those who have to cope with meetings and appointments. However, time control is something every person will deal with no matter the mission, scenario, or job.

Advantages of time control

Time management is the use of time efficaciously by using utilizing it skillfully when it's far available. It is able to permit people to do the proper matters at the right time. Time management plays a large position in human beings' expert and personal lives, and on this aggressive global, time is a vital issue, therefore, humans ought to be gifted sufficient on the subject of time management, understanding that it's miles very vital and ought to not be taken for granted. Time management has many advantages, but failure to manage time can impact a person's expert and private lifestyles negatively. Some of the blessings encompass pressure level discount, provision of awareness on a project, procrastination decrease, self-assurance, economic soundness, and provides rest and leisure sports time.

Time management can assist reduce folks' pressure ranges and can bring about the achievements of one's dreams inside specific cut-off dates. Decreasing strain is an advantage of time control, and people who manipulate their time successfully usually be triumphant at responsibilities and are less confused. Time control additionally leads to economic benefits; today, cash is one of the factors that is used to degree success. Someone will become financially sound if she or he has planned his or her lifestyles well and maintains a timetable of his or her professional and personal existence. Planning is straightforward, however, obeying a plan calls for discipline and powerful time control. Self-belief is also executed because of time control. It performs a giant function in human's lifestyles; self-assured people have a tendency to have a higher lifestyle than folks that are depending on others. Time control does not take a person's time, but it creates more time for someone. Persons who manage time nicely will excel, and their self-trust can make them achieve. Time management can assist to put off procrastination. It does now not need any greater or special competencies, the simplest component it requires is expertise about the way to and the implementation dedication inside the day after day activities. Procrastination is one of the factors that negatively affect fulfillment. But, time management permits humans to decrease it. Additionally, time control offers to focus on duties. Persons who are targeted have greater possibilities of becoming a success, compared to humans who aren't targeted. All people have a preference to reach existence; however, it's miles less complicated stated than executed. People need to need fulfillment and be dedicated and manipulate time accurately so that their dreams may be found out.

Chapter Five

Literacy and Social Interaction

Studies have supplied a few fascinating examples of the distinctive issues faced with the aid of excessive ability college students with studying disabilities and reimbursement strategies used to addressing and overcoming demanding situations associated with specific studying disabilities. Many academically gifted young human beings with learning disabilities never qualify for programs for gifted and gifted freshmen and fail to reach college however those who do learn strategies that help them to prevail, regardless of their mastering problems. We will be looking at three (3) compensatory and remedial applications applied in an inclusive putting. Compensatory & Remedial packages carried out into Inclusive Settings. The purpose of compensatory education is grounded within the exercise of addressing the effects of poverty on getting to know and teaching. There is an assumption that scholars from low-profit populations were manufactured from low investment in housing, nutrition, schooling inside the domestic. Compensatory schooling is meant to provide additional investment in human capital for low-income students to make amends for the higher investment in human capital afforded to the more advantaged populace. Reyes (2006) cited the reimbursement techniques as a broad magnificence of gaining knowledge of strategies that "describe examine, cognitive, spatial, reminiscence, or studying strategies", and explained that students with learning disabilities use compensation techniques because they provide powerful methods for processing records while questioning, remembering, storing and making sense of vintage and new records. Student education may be likened to constructing a residence till the muse is laid, this is while the second floor of the building will begin. Remedial coaching targets the foundational competencies walking Head: Compensatory & Remedial packages implemented into Inclusive Settings a baby needs to grasp, this is essential to assist the kid progress with extra advanced standards and abilities. Some remedial procedures include re-coaching skills and the usage of special coaching methods that shape the scholar's learning needs, breaking down the task right into a smaller bite. Summer season applications also can be endorsed for the child, it has to do with constructing the scholar's strength and working around the weak point. Audiobooks, a text-speech software program can offer alternative approaches to gaining knowledge for students with unique wishes. Keep in mind that the use of compensatory tactics doesn't imply your child has to prevent receiving remedial instruction. Locating the proper balance between remediation and compensatory strategies is crucial. For many kids with studying and wondering differences, it's quality to goal for a combo. Remedial preparation will cope with competencies deficits at the same time as compensatory strategies will permit them to reach their complete capability. Specific principles to assess the advantage of compensatory and remedial packages for diverse newcomers in teaching strategies, nobody length in shape all method on any situation. Analyzing and writing have reached a stage of range in the lecture room, in this instance, variety manner human distinction. some great strategies or standards for meeting the wishes of diverse students are; differentiated coaching, culturally responsive coaching and last fulfillment gap through enrichment differentiated preparation differentiating instructions is one of the nice ways to make sure students of different degrees all get their desires met. The teacher thinks of differentiation as making training on hand on multiple stages and presenting opportunities for each pupil to work on their character wishes. The teacher jogging Head: Compensatory & Remedial applications implemented into Inclusive Settings differentiates by using having small corporations for studying and writing training even as ensuring there may be suitable independent work for different college students to do at the same time as he focuses on his small organization. He also differentiates by offering visual aids to students who gain from image organizers, at the same time as challenging more independent college students to work without such scaffolds. He previews his training along with his neediest college students so they get extra time to grasp difficult principles and new vocabulary. The teacher also makes certain his most superior readers and writers are always challenged to study more complex texts and write extra state-of-the-art pieces. Differentiation takes time, especially inside the making plans levels, but it pays off due to the fact college students are greater engaged when they are able to work exactly at their level. Culturally Responsive teaching the instructor additionally is aware that potential is not the simplest issue of range gift whilst he teaches literacy. The cultural variety of his elegance has a sturdy effect on how he teaches studying and writing. The teacher tries to exercise culturally responsive pedagogy or coaching that keeps in mind his students' backgrounds and previous expertise. Some of the approaches that cultural responsiveness comes into play all through literacy instruction include: closing the success gap with enrichment. The enrichment technique is consistent with outcomes that stepped forward student achievement and reduction and achievement among the rich and the negative and among specific ethnic corporations. The faculty development process usually starts with a radical evaluation of the strengths and weaknesses of all dimensions of the college, which ends up inside the advent of a college mission, a strategic plan with extensive instructional goals, particular studying goals, and particular movement plans as revealed by using Beecher & Sweeny (2008). Jogging Head: Compensatory & Remedial programs applied into Inclusive Settings conclusion instructors ought to layout appropriate studying sports in step with the point of interest of coaching. Based totally on the low start line, small steps, diversified sports, and instantaneous remarks, teachers have to inspire students to participate actively during the getting to know the technique to assist grasp the capabilities and methods of collaborative studying. different teaching sports consisting of situational coaching, competitions, collation of facts, dialogue, oral reporting, video games, topical research, production of graphs/figures/models, function play, recording, go to and experiments can also help pupils beautify their interest in learning, stimulate their questioning and make stronger the effectiveness of teaching. Instructors ought to exercise their discretion in the appropriate use of coaching aids. Suitable teaching aids, not the most effective assist to beautify student interest in getting to know however will even consolidate the expertise they found out, thereby reaching the objective of coaching. Going for walks Head: Compensatory & Remedial programs applied into Inclusive Settings References.

Despite the intersection of the extraordinary gaining knowledge of environments that targets to benefit college students, it may have implications. One in everything that's the reality of now not pleasurable the wishes of all college students. The desires of every network are different and it is surprisingly impossible to design substances and instructions to person college students. For this reason, as an instructor, we would permit students to make recommendations and supply thoughts that may be implemented so all can benefit. Assessment is one way wherein to provide clear indicators of how students are progressing academically. It is a critical piece of the getting-to-know manner. It is a key component of coaching and getting to know because it enhances mastering but at the equal time affords applicable records for teaching. Ronan (2015) defines assessment as the dimension of what college students are studying. He further elaborated that the assessment gives educators with each objective and subjective data so one can ascertain pupil progress and talent mastery. The information whether or not it is qualitative or quantitative collected from the assessment is extraordinarily treasured as it units the platform for a system that complements each coaching and gaining knowledge of. Assessment is no longer seen as become independent from teaching and mastering however as an indispensable factor of the technique. This essay will speak the results of formative assessment to teachers in addition to the scholar in any schoolroom. First off, a formative assessment discusses that formative assessments are genuinely gear which is wished through teachers to decide how college students are progressing via a sure studying goal." It lets the trainer monitors scholar performance and development in the course of study. This form of learning is regularly low-stakes and ungraded. It's used as a manner for the trainer to look if the student is making development towards the quit goal of learning the talent. The number one reason for evaluation for me as a Mathematics instructor is to inform and improve the teaching and mastering of mathematics. A formative assessment like a weekly take a look at, quizzes, worksheets, and sophistication dialogue can provide precious facts at the depth of know-how and talent degree of each student. Getting access to this information can allow the trainer to plan, alter or modify the training to make sure that the objectives of the unit are completely grasped and attained by way of the scholars. Instructors may be in a very good role to make applicable academic choices to facilitate college students learning. That is supported through the Western and FORMATIVE assessment Northern Canadian Protocol for Collaboration in education that formative evaluation is designed to give instructors facts to alter and differentiate teaching and mastering sports. The steady and sustained formative evaluation also allows instructors to evaluate the effectiveness of their coaching.

Regions of weak spots or misconceptions may be retaught and additional instructional sports are designed to foster and expand college students' expertise. However, the announcement, 'formative tests are formative for students' means that scholars need to at the least showcase or display in a behavioral manner their understanding of the ideas taught inside the class. Sadler (1989, p.7) argues that it encompasses classroom interactions, questioning, established schoolroom activities, and feedback aimed at assisting students to shut mastering gaps. Students also are actively worried inside the assessment process via self and peer-assessment. It specializes in the position of the scholar as the critical connector among assessment and learning. In line with Western and Northern Canadian Protocol for Collaboration in education. "While college students are energetic, engaged, and vital assessors, they make sense of records, relate it to prior know-how, and use it for brand new gaining knowledge of." The formative evaluation also presents a very good performance indicator and remarks gear for college students. It occurs when students monitor their own getting to know and use the comments from this monitoring to make modifications, diversifications, and even fundamental changes in what they apprehend. A study with the aid of the Black and William evaluation noted through Sadler (1989, p.eight) also determined that formative assessment techniques were, in a few cases, particularly effective for lower-accomplishing students, therefore decreasing inequity of student outcomes and elevating average achievement. This approach "FORMATIVE evaluation" allows college students to interact in an aware mirrored image of the studying process, properly. In my mathematics elegance, college students can definitely discover areas that need reinforcement with respect to ability degrees, talent, and ordinary knowledge. Students will then use the remarks from the tests in collaboration with the teacher to set revision and additional educational activities that concentrate on the preferred abilities that need to be evolved. In conclusion, formative evaluation is critical as a shape of feedback to inform each instructor and college student of the effectiveness of preparation and studying inside the lecture room. Teachers want to be greater systematic in their technique to study room assessment, as the simplest interactions with students are the end result of cautious planning. The best of formative evaluation rests, in part, on strategies instructors use to elicit evidence of students getting to know related to desires, with the right stage of the element to shape subsequent coaching.

Evaluation is essential to college students' learning, and college students' evaluation refers to methods in which proof of learning is accumulated in a planned and systematic way which will make a judgment approximately pupil learning. it's far a fundamental part of the coaching and studying method and it is described as a technique of accumulating, describing, or quantifying facts approximately scholar performance. It is a form of a well-designed check which can act as an engine that eventually derives active scholar learning. Additionally, it performs an extensive function in studying regardless of the environment, traditional or online and well-known principles are comparable in each environment. Moreover, assessment plays a sizable role in gaining knowledge regardless of the environment; formative. Summative or traditional and the overall ideas have variation and similarities within the environments. The environmental elements at a school will have an impact on learning and the type of problems and sports students interact in, be it nice or bad. If the surroundings are terrible, college students will stumble upon various problems and problems that could result in them becoming frustrated, even as losing attention and hobby. They may experience cognitive problems which encompass failure to evolve mentally to what they may be experiencing. This will have an effect on their performance, and it is able to bring about them reaching decrease grades.

Formative, summative and conventional assessments are a number of the most kinds of exams within the academic device, and in spite of their variations and similarities, they serve their very own purpose. Formative assessment focuses on the enhancement of instructors' and college students' studying, summative evaluation specializes in the consequences and results and traditional assessment focuses on the layout of exams.

Formative assessments cater to both the teachers via supplying them with the relevant records that are had to enhance their learning journey and its system. Its cause is to help form, or form, a scholar's mastering during the studying manner, which demands administration and scoring. pupil formative evaluation, or evaluation for getting to know, objectives to pick out aspects of learning as it's miles growing in an effort to deepen and shape subsequent getting to know, and at the same time as now, not a "silver bullet" that may solve all instructional challenges, it offers an effective means for assembly dreams for excessive-performance, high-equity of scholar outcomes, and for imparting students with understanding and talents for lifelong gaining knowledge of systems. .Black and William (1998) outline formative evaluation as the sports taken by means of teachers to provide remarks on what the scholars have simply completed. Popham (2008) regards it as a designed plan to adjust the continuing getting to know the procedure.

Summative exams are generally administered to college students at the stop of an educational school time period and are administered at the cease of each term at some point of the school year. Certainly one of its not unusual goals of assessing students is to degree the mastery of learning standards. Scholar summative evaluation or assessment of gaining knowledge of, targets to summarize gaining knowledge of that has taken location, with the intention to file, mark or certify achievements.

Traditional assessment consists of strategies such as more than one desire test, authentic-fake statements; fill in the gaps, and matching physical games irrelevant for the foreign language lecture room curricula. They point out the lack of wealth, descriptive information about each product, and manner of gaining knowledge of conventional checking out methods used for measuring students' expertise. Its motive is to evaluate the students' level of training, to determine if they're maintaining statistics given by means of the teachers so that a grade may be assigned to them based on their performance, and to measure their work and evaluate them towards standards the learning group and different students.

Despite the fact that checks are presently used for many purposes inside the instructional device, the fact is that their effectiveness and utility must in the long run be judged by the volume to which they promote college students' learning. The intention of assessments needs to be to educate and improve students' performance, no longer merely to audit it. From every assessment, it's miles crucial that each instructor and college students learn from the enjoy, and it's far crucial to be aware that get the right of entry to statistics is valid, dependable, and correct helps to encourage properly informed choices. Information this is received needs to be put to correct use through informing selections approximately curriculum and education and in the end improving students' getting to know, Falk (2000) and countrywide Council of teachers of arithmetic (1995).

Samples of checks that align with the quality practices consist of:

(a)   Remember to recognize identification; a sample of this evaluation is:

Select the most appropriate phrase to finish the sentence Query:

1.   Elements of a tree are the trunk, branches, and ------------ (toes, head, roots)

2.   The color of a carrot is:

a.   Crimson

b.   Blue

c.   Orange

d.   Red

3.   Remember four (four) key phrases that are utilized by behavioral theorists

(b)   Interpret, Summarize, compare and explain. A sample of this evaluation is:

1.   Provide an explanation for the which means of the time period curriculum

2.   Summarize the concept of the film Black Panther

3.   Examine and comparison two (2) Social mastering Theories

4.   Supply your interpretation of the magnificence undertaking

(c)   Practice, Execute, put in force. A pattern of this evaluation is:

1.   Apply one instructional precept to a classroom setting

2.   Execute a disaster plan for the elegance

3.   Enforce three (3) techniques to address bullying

Techniques of pleasant exercise

True coaching practice is a key influence on pupils getting to know - a desired outcome and primary goal of better educational establishments. Instructors attempt to meet the standards of proper exercise on the way to provide a pleasant studying enjoy for his or her students. Strategies at the nice practices listing and their educational merit consist of:

•   Instructors promoting top verbal exchange among instructors and rookies

•   Encouraging interaction amongst inexperienced persons

•   Presenting possibilities for energetic participation among students

•   Permitting timely and suitable reaction and comments

•   Emphasizing allotted time on the project

• Motivating gaining knowledge of through speaking expectancies
• Respecting numerous capabilities and approaches of mastering

Those concepts of alignment require that all components of the curriculum should be aligned for maximum effect on pupils gaining knowledge. The benefit of those practices is in keeping with the technical elements of classroom assessment. However, there are consequences to assessments; each lengthy-time period and quick-time period requires teachers to have an ethical obligation to make selections that are the most valid and reliable as viable. The assessment strategies on the best practices list intention to facilitate learning; wherein, checks provide proof of college students getting to know outcomes. The techniques of assessment also give evidence of how learners are progressing according to defined standards at some point of a length of studying, in addition to achievement on the stop of the gaining knowledge of duration.

Teachers play an important role in the way students broaden and the manner wherein their behavior is shaped. Having a hit academic revel in may be stricken by the expectation and belief of the lecturers. The behavior of instructors has an amazing influence and impact on students' studying consequences, because of the truth that they depend on teachers for guidance and to encourage them to carry out. Teachers' behavior toward college students can have negative and advantageous results on students and it can close for a completely long time. Based on studies, it was surmised that excessive teacher expectation implies that the trainer accepts as true that the scholars are high-achiever and the dynamics sell growth and development. Gaining knowledge is defined through the Merriam-Webster dictionary as "an interest or manner of gaining expertise or ability by means of reading, training, being taught, or experiencing something or as the hobby of someone who learns". Additionally, states that mastering is intentionally coming to recognize as a result of experience. Whilst instructors have expectations of college students, they have an effect on mastering by means of providing what's important for the classroom to facilitate and encourage getting to know.

Teachers also play a vast position in the enhancement of 21st Century competencies, by using focusing on the standards which might be geared closer to total development. With the mixing of recent technology, and a well-designed curriculum, together with the expertise of teachers, students will be able to research in a twenty-first-century context, and once those concepts are properly utilized, collectively they will offer healthy learning surroundings. a number of the concepts of the 21st Century are: that specialize in core topics, emphasizing interdisciplinary mastering, incorporating the twenty-first-century equipment, coaching and getting to know the 21st-century content material, and assessing newbies in rigorous and applicable approaches. The 21st Century equipment encompasses one-of-a-kind versions of technology that may be challenging for many teachers at the beginning. Studies show that many instructors are unusual with twenty-first Century competencies and academic technology. Assessment of quality practices in coaching and gaining knowledge of, 21st Century capabilities take root when teachers: 1. begin with actual-global issues and tactics 2. Assist inquiry-based learning studies 3. Offer opportunities for collaborative challenge work 4. Emphasize how to examine (i.e., above what to examine). The twenty-first Century has a super effect on my belief about teaching; many accept as true with that so as to get the maximum out of students, we must increase the banner of success.

 I like the incorporation of the era within the study room; this helps in aiding within the information and the development of students. These skills are very important for college kids to research and achieve success. But, many agree that the vital gaining knowledge of and Innovation abilities are most crucial; students need to accumulate the abilities which might be required so as for them to achieve success. Trilling and Fadel agree that communique and collaboration are important ingredients for career achievement. precise significance is the ability to articulate thoughts definitely, to listen efficiently, to make use of more than one media, and to work correctly and respectfully in diverse teams, Trilling and Fadel (2009. crucial questioning and problem fixing continue to be salient property for learners and career seekers, they may be additionally given a new dimension in the 21st century via superior technology for accessing, studying, and growing facts.

They additionally agree that creativity and innovation are vital to the extent to which research, apprehend and carry out tasks. Pupils advise creativity can be developed over the years in an equal way as other talents. It's very critical for college kids to research and explicit their area of expertise; that is step one in developing their private logo that is what they will be diagnosed by using and be reputable for. a few factors that make contributions to a man or woman's happiness are social relationships, temperament version, money, society and subculture, and tremendous wondering styles.

There are numerous not unusual triggers for anger, such as losing your patience, feeling as if your opinion or efforts aren't favored, and also injustice. Other causes of anger consist of recollections of demanding or enraging events and disturbing private problems.

Worry is an emotion brought on by way of perceived threat or hazard, which reasons physiological modifications and in the long run behavioral modifications, such as fleeing, hiding, or freezing from perceived traumatic activities. Whilst a person sees something that frightens them, like a big spider, their amygdala is activated and, in turn, turns on other areas of the mind, particularly the hypothalamus. The hypothalamus then triggers the discharge of hormones, including adrenaline, that's responsible for our "combat or flight" reaction.

Unhappiness is one of the four human emotions. The others being happiness, fear, and anger. It is legitimate and useful and alerts us to how we need to deal with ourselves, and also as to how we want to be dealt with with the aid of others.

Being sad should now not be pressured with melancholy (malignant sadness) or grief. We also grow to be sad while a person we love is unkind to us, while we see or enjoy something poignant. Unhappiness is likewise while we experience some loss or harm. When we are angry, the underlying emotion is both unhappiness and fear.

Our moves are one of a kind from our emotions but they're very strongly prompted by way of them. One manner that our moves are affected by feelings is through motivation, which drives someone's moves. Feelings can also affect our actions immediately, as in the case of aggression, or actions that is centered on hurting others Your emotions will drive the decisions you're making today, and your fulfillment may additionally depend on your capacity to recognize and interpret them. Whilst an emotion is induced on your mind, your anxious machine responds with the aid of creating feelings on your body (what many people consult with as an "intestine feeling") and sure mind on your mind.

Is low self-esteem an excellent predictor of violent behavior and a contribution to literacy troubles? Low shallowness leads to violent conduct. Common expertise has long held that low shallowness leads to numerous antisocial behaviors, together with violent behavior. Low self-esteem and self-confidence are discovered amongst victims of violence. Low vanity can get us to make self-unfavorable selections which include tolerating mistreatment or harming ourselves (by using tablets, becoming promiscuous.

Is mental contamination a good predictor of violent behavior?
Untreated mental infection because persons been arrested for risky and violent behavior. People with severe mental

contamination are victimized by means of violent acts greater regularly than they dedicate violent acts. Maximum acts of violence are dedicated by using folks that are not mentally unwell. Maximum individuals with psychiatric issues aren't violent. Even though a subset of humans with psychiatric issues commit assaults and violent crimes.

What is intellectual illness?

Mental illness is a condition that influences someone's thinking, feeling, or mood. Such situations might also have an effect on someone's ability to relate to others and feature each day. Anybody may have extraordinary stories, even human beings with the same prognosis. Intellectual illness, additionally known as intellectual fitness disorders, refers to a huge range of intellectual health conditions, issues that have an effect on your temper, questioning, and conduct. Examples of mental infection consist of despair, tension disorders, schizophrenia, ingesting problems, and addictive behaviors. Intellectual contamination can make you miserable and may reason problems in your day-by-day life, along with at school or work or in relationships. In maximum cases, signs can be controlled with an aggregate of medicinal drugs and talk remedy (psychotherapy).

Humans with kind A persona are said to have an increased danger of illnesses which include pressure-related heart disorder. Yet, when they fill out the Social Readjustment Rating Scale, their scores are regularly low. Why might that scale underestimate the pressure levels of kinda people? Humans with kind A character people usually consciousness extra on themselves and are greater introverted because of their competitive tendencies consistent with studies. They also appear to want to have a terrific repute in society; they may be additionally very competitive and they placed mores pressure on themselves which cause them to sick and so, their end result is disrupted.

Study room putting and mastering

Schoolroom seating association for college students is common of outstanding price, and it has amazing effects on students and their studying. It's far important for teachers to configure their school rooms to their likeness, their specific fashion, and in a manner so that it will serve each of them and the scholars properly. While a lecture room design is according to the teacher's style of teaching, he/she can provide presentations and teachers with authority, strength, and self-assurance and it is also finished with excessive clarity and as an end result, the scholars gain greatly. When configuring lecture rooms, there are numerous factors that need to be taken into consideration which encompass: lecture room length and form, the level of distraction and its route, the size and in a few instances, the age of the students, and the trainer's teaching style and his/her study room objectives.

 Earlier than you readjust a lecture room, as an instructor, you want to don't forget the amount of space that is to be had whilst maintaining in thoughts the region of furniture and try to keep away from all and sundry getting harm. Instructors additionally need to take into account the classrooms' distractions and try and minimize them as a lot as feasible because distractions restrict students' gaining knowledge. Distractions can be little things that get the eye of college students and stopping them from paying attention to what is being taught. The dimensions of a category must be carefully considered and the long time of the scholars. In many situations, you discover the younger college students are the ones that are extra without difficulty distracted, in order that they want to be positioned in regions that they are able to have regular eye touch with the lecturers. But, for coaching to be effective, a lecture room doesn't need to be configured, the academics just ought to find innovative ways to teach. The teaching fashion and school room targets are most effective to me on the subject of coaching. Based totally on what instructors are hoping to acquire within the lecture rooms will motivate them to do their high quality, giving each scholar an incredible possibility to prevail.

As a teacher, the numerous lecture room seating arrangements of your choice for the students will have high-quality and terrible feedback and many impacts on the dynamics of the entire classroom. Three lecture room styles are Clusters, U-shape, and conventional rows. Clusters normally facilitate group work and allow less complicated navigation inside the lecture room, however, the bad thing of such putting is the fact that now not all the students can be capable of face the trainer that could reason some college students to be distracted and distract others. The U-shape arrangement decreases many schoolroom challenges and allows the instructor to effortlessly move thru the classroom and captivate the attention of the students. However, with such putting, the dynamics of companies and institution work may be declined to a wonderful quantity especially if the magnificence has a large variety of students. Conventional

Row configuration is known as the most not unusual study room association. This sort of putting works nicely with many class structures which can be according to an instructor/scholar-based curriculum. With this setting, college students are greater at risk of gaining knowledge of, extra organized and attention and it could work with any study room length. however, this putting too has its negative aspect; whilst this format is used, maximum of the students that take part in schoolroom activities are those who are seated at the front and the middle, even as those seated at the again shy away.

In keeping with the academic communication idea, the physical setup of chairs, tables, and presentation in a classroom can drastically have an impact on mastering, and the seating arrangements can impact how the teacher communicates with students and how the students interact with one another, impacting engagement, motivation, and attention. Harvey and Kenyon in a recent study also advise that students tend to decide on more flexible seating arrangements. Many opt for the conventional rows due to the truth that it accommodates the specific magnificence sizes. They consider that established rules, mastering may be carried out despite the few demanding situations faced.

A study room environment may be very important to get to know the final results and development of children. It ought to be one this is pupil pleasant and promotes gaining knowledge of. It is the region in which instructors affect the behavior of students that will broaden, excel and reap their academic dreams. Inside the schoolroom, students learn how to form fantastic relationships; research the fee of teamwork as well as running independently, voice their opinions, apprehend the benefits of collaboration and also find out their strengths and weaknesses. The classroom surroundings serve as a human development centre where the point of interest is on the holistic improvement of the scholars, allowing them the opportunity to stay their full ability. This is where students spend most of their time with their teachers as they analyze the vital abilities which is beneficial and allows them in achieving their mastering targets.

However, within the study room, there have to be set up guidelines and methods that will decorate getting to know. Without regulations inside the lecture room, there can be no order and the classroom might be disorganized, and getting to know could be affected significantly. Rules also help instructors to area college students and educate them on responsibility and strength of mind, therefore, policies must be bolstered regularly.

Primarily based on the regulations and procedures which can be used in the lecture room can either sell and beautify studying or avert the classroom's objectives, therefore, instructors want to consider in their approach when growing and setting policies inside the lecture room as have a superb or bad effect on the students and they're getting to know effects. For regulations and processes to create fantastic lecture room environments and that should be clear, clean to recognize, and consider, they should aim to create order within the lecture room and that they ought to be in accordance with the college's policy. They need to be normally truthful to the students even as addressing their desires and need to be easily enforceable and they have to satisfy the scholars' parents. Teachers additionally need to certainly give an explanation for to the scholars what's predicted of them and the outcomes for no longer adhering to the regulations. It needs to not be expected for students to exchange their behavior mechanically, and because of such, the processes and techniques that teachers may additionally use inside the lecture room ought to empower students to do better. There are simple things that can be performed to put into effect those rules which include instructors imparting each pupil with a list of the policies to take domestic so that their parents will be aware of them, and sticking up a list of the guidelines on the walls of the study room. Also, teachers could have the scholars write down the rules of their books and then speak them with them so that they will apprehend.

From my revel in, they agree that when the gaining knowledge of surroundings is high quality, the gaining knowledge of consequences of college students are also superb. According to helping writers, college students analyze better once they view the gaining knowledge of surroundings as fine and supportive. A wonderful surrounding is one in which students sense a feeling of belonging, trust others, and experience recommended to address demanding situations, take risks, and ask questions. Such an environment gives relevant content material, clean learning dreams and comments, opportunities to construct social competencies, and strategies to assist college students to prevail. A few kinds of rules within the schoolroom have to be encouraged and a few must be discouraged due to the truth that some make wonderful contributions and others poor ones. People who make a contribution undoubtedly need to be bolstered as they affect the scholars' lives and help them to obtain fulfillment. Alternatively, the ones who might be poor should be discouraged due to the fact they will have an effect on getting to know negatively and will deprive them from succeeding academically and in any other case. While rules are created and are determined inside the lecture room, teachers can understand if they might have created wonderful or negative study room surroundings.

Classroom discipline could be very critical to the development of college students and it teaches them to create the structure of their lives and be organized. Many theorists emphasized its importance and discussed numerous approaches that can be carried out and performed into the lecture room for greater high-quality gaining knowledge of the outcome.

Linda evolved an approach known as the Cooperate subject. This method turned designed to use inside the schoolroom and allow teachers to meet the needs of every student by using distinctive techniques. Those techniques will even help college students to turn out to be conscious of their behavior and be able to adjust it in which vital. Teachers cannot change students' behavior, they can most effectively impact them. Albert's Cooperate area centered on three (three) forms of the area; corrective area, preventative discipline, and supportive area. These disciplines study the holistic improvement of students and their ordinary behavior and they assist college students to hook up with every different at the same time as feeling an experience of belonging and increase their self-assurance. Via making use of her approach inside the study room, it will remodel the study room by giving each pupil and possibility to excel as they come to be extra aware and well known their capabilities.

Kegan, then again, designed his technique referred to as

Win-Win discipline which is powerful to the study room. Its layout centered on ways in which to handle troubles in the schoolroom with the aid of using different problem-solving techniques. The Win-Win subject will pay near attention on the basis cause of issues so an answer can be found. This area additionally makes a specialty of positions; there are seven (7) positions that make up this area. They're, the attention searching for function, the avoiding embarrassment role, and the anger venting role, the control in search of a role, the energetic function, the board function, and the uninformed function. It's important for teachers to recognize college students' positions in an effort to interact with them in non-disruptive behaviors and applications.

Both theorists are seeking to broaden college students and beautify their behavior; they provide instructors with techniques that can be used to transform school rooms. They each focus on the holistic improvement and the getting to know outcomes of college students. Theories are there to guide teachers in decision-making and to educate them on the extraordinary strategies that they could use inside the study room. Theories may be carried out to all ages and could provide amazing advantages. The tools that can be used for building personal and create positive outputs in every issue of existence.

Albert and Kegan had not unusual desires and that they each took into attention, the destiny generations, and so, they designed their strategies in a way that may be used at present, as well as within the destiny, at the same time as having equal advantages to people. Despite the fact that they each had not unusual goals, additionally, they had extraordinary thoughts on a way to cope with the behavior of students and lecture room control. However, despite their specific methods and approaches, they each aim to bring about an efficient lecture room. Albert and Kegan consist of diverse capabilities and techniques of their tactics for the reason of subject.

Albert's technique targeted at the correction and support of students by the academics, but it teaches students to save you issues, while Kegan emphasized the dealing with of issues. They are key elements that assist to shape and discipline college students to end up as better versions of themselves for school and society. Those techniques are student-targeted and allow teachers to be bendy of their execution.

Chapter Six

Social Skills

Social talents are very vital to our improvement; they're numerous abilities that we use to speak efficiently and engage with others, verbally and non-verbally, via one-of-a-kind gestures, body language, and our non-public being. People were uniquely created and we had been made to socialize, therefore, we're sociable beings and we've got advanced the skill of effective communique and we exhibit such via our messages, mind, and emotions to each other. "Social competencies" embody quite a number of unique skills that are interrelated. Simply by means of practicing one type of social skill, you may improve in different regions, but it enables you to be aware of as many of them as feasible. Social abilities are defined as socially desirable styles of conduct that permit students to gain social reinforcement and acceptance and keep away from aversive social situations. They state that good enough social improvement is the inspiration of personal and social adjustment in existence. They also provide proof that deficits in social abilities are connected to negative social adjustments, mental health issues, delinquency, and occasional self-esteem. Poor social skills are believed to be related to the following elements: 1-restricted possibilities to study; two bad instructional and social self-concept; and three social isolation. Most importantly social capabilities are specific, identifiable, discrete, found out behaviors with a purpose to bring about the true interplay among humans.

Schooling in social abilities has multiple components to assure its fulfillment and nice results. Any other instance of institution initiatives is giving thank you all through a specific duration and the intention is to educate the ability to say "thanks" or "thank you" whilst someone does something fine for them. Some other examples of group tasks are to mirror the things for which we are grateful and the purpose right here is to allow students to reflect on the fantastic matters in their lives. Vacation items are another amazing instance for group projects and thru this students are to mirror their strengths. The new decision is another institution venture for students to set and attain dreams for the month. begin every day with a smile is a collection task that stresses the significance of a smile and the superb impact a grin may have on the scholar himself and on the ones around him.

Whether a pupil is a social butterfly or a bonafide wallflower, their personal social abilities can relatively have an effect on extra than whom they're taking to promenade. In unique, there may be a correlated relationship between how a student interacts with their friends and instructors in mixture with how receptive and educationally flexible they're. Bearing this in thoughts, there may be tons to look at concerning social talents when one is searching out enhancements in nowadays educational efficiency. To explicate, it is critical to keep in mind that social abilities are simply standards of public interactions that still influence how successfully a pupil can attention to mastering and is resultantly a subject that deserves extra interest inside the classroom that it's presently receiving. To reiterate, social skills are the maximum primary abilities from which a person behaves with other people. Mainly, these skills act as inner equations that compute responses, depending on variables along with the setting, the connection among people, and concern. in particular, authors and psychologists advocate that the five predominant regions of social capabilities are peer relational talents, self-control abilities, academic abilities, compliance capabilities, and statement abilities.

Therefore, the character of what social capabilities are and the common formation of interpersonal relationships in school rooms cast absolute confidence at the truth that the social-ness and mastering strongly correlate. To this stop, the substantial capability to enhance these days and day after today's gaining knowledge of conditions need to be addressed by means of the usage of what is known and researching what is but to be recognized about the connection between social interactions. On the entirety of the problem, to be social is human conduct, and to be social inside the study room is studious

What we are saying motivated by verbal language and with the aid of manner we use it; the tone of voice, the volume of speech, and our choice of words, in addition to by way of greater diffused messages which encompass body language, gestures, and other non-verbal conversation methods. The reality is that a few people are higher social interactors than others and this has brought about designated investigations into the character of interpersonal interactions. Growing social abilities is set being aware of how we speak greater green and effective. There are awesome advantages to having properly advanced social skills. They consist of:

• Extra and higher relationships; identifying properly with a person leads to greater relationships and, at times, friendships. Via growing your social competencies, you emerge as extra charismatic, a proper trait. Humans are greater interested in charismatic people than charismatic people are or as a minimum appear to be more interested in them. The general public realizes which you can't advance some distance in existence without sturdy interpersonal relationships. Consequently, focusing on relationships will assist you to get a process, get promotions and make want pals. Properly-honed social talents can boom your happiness and satisfaction and give you a better outlook on lifestyles. Greater relationships also can help to lessen the poor effects of stress and increase your self-esteem.

• Higher communication; relating with human beings and being able to work in large companies obviously expand one's verbal exchange abilities. in any case, you can have excellent social capabilities without precise conversation talents, and being capable of delivering one's thoughts and ideas can be the unmarried maximum essential ability that you can broaden in lifestyles.

• Greater performance; after you are correct with people, you could without problems avoid being with the people you do not partner yourself with. Some humans dread social interactions because they do not wish to spend time with those who do not have comparable hobbies and viewpoints. It is a lot less complicated to attend a meeting at work or a party on your personal lifestyle if you understand some of the humans that might be there. if you are in a social situation and do now not need to spend time with a specific man or woman due to the fact you don't just like the character or because he/she cannot help you with a selected difficulty, a very good set of social abilities will let you with politeness convey that you want to spend time with other people at the get-together.

• Advancing career prospects; maximum profitable jobs have a 'human's element' and the most lucrative positions frequently involve a huge amount of time spent interacting with employees, media, and co-workers. It is rare that a man or woman can continue to be isolated from their workplace and nevertheless excel in their task. Maximum businesses are seeking out individuals with a particular, tactical, skillset; the potential to work properly in a group, and to influence and encourage human beings to get things performed.

• Elevated universal Happiness; getting along and know-how people will help to open many personal and profession-associated doorways. Having the confidence to begin a verbal exchange at a piece-related convention may additionally result in a new activity provide with a better income. a smile in a social state of affairs can also lead to a friendship being formed.

Traits of Social skills
• Social capabilities are intention-directed.
• Social professional behaviors are interrelated inside the

feel that one person may also use more than one kind of behavior at the same time and for an equal purpose.

• Social abilities have to be suitable to the state of affairs of verbal exchange. Extraordinary social talents might be used for professional and private communication.

• Social abilities may be diagnosed as positive styles of behavior wherein a person may be judged on how socially skilled they're.

• Social capabilities can be taught, practiced, and learned.

• Social abilities have to be underneath the cognitive management of the individual- learning them involves getting to know while to use unique behaviors, as well as what behaviors to use or a way to use them.

The importance of social competencies

One teacher stated, "We start every consultation at school by way of taking five minutes and getting students to speak". We virtually ask, "What have you been as much as considering that we noticed you ultimately?" This smooth query and hobby is exceedingly hard for plenty of college students, that is precisely why we do it. The trouble is, current training and society have made social skill acquisition more difficult than ever earlier. In Taiwan, where we are based, students spend almost all of their waking hours in a study room taking note of instructors and taking tests. If they are not in the faculty or doing homework, there is a good chance students are looking at a screen of some type. The quantity of time students spend actively interacting with each other is tiny, so even among their friends, scholar social talents are lacking. However, the modern-day international additionally requires interaction not simply with friends, but with instructors, different adults, or even people from one-of-a-kind countries. How is a scholar intended to meaningfully have interaction with so many distinctive varieties of people while all of their time is consumed by faculty and smartphones?

Medical doctors see masses of sufferers a day, attorneys spend a whole lot of their time negotiating, explaining, and convincing others, and CEOs are tasked with constructing green and dynamic groups, which lead them to achievement. Social skills – the potential to talk, have interaction, make buddies, convince others, and gain belief – are perhaps more crucial than another set of talents. However, in place of trying to foster these in students, we've deeply restrained them.

This is why faculties have to make social talents a concern. College students need to talk in magnificence. They need to suppose of things to mention. They want to learn to have interaction with their instructors – adults from distinct international locations who do matters differently than mother and father or local teachers. whilst our heat-up sessions are vital, they may be also only the beginning; writing schooling demands that scholars open up, bear in mind their thoughts, and learn to explicit them capably, first to teachers, then to everybody else. In reality, we stay in a world wherein verbal exchange and social capabilities are increasingly more crucial. As such, we cause them to a priority, and you should too.

Talking and communication
Having the ability to talk whilst spoken to maybe a tall

order for a shy student, and for apparent motives, however, it is deeply essential. Even asking a student "how are you these days" can elicit nothing but blank stares, and youngsters (and adults!) want to recover from this. It's true, from time to time students don't apprehend while someone is talking to them, however, they should say that rather than freeze.

Beyond simply responding and being able to talk, college students also want to discover ways to engage in a communique. Let's cross again to our heat-up workout: we ask students what they did over the weekend or the day prior to this or whatever. College students frequently respond with, "nothing," and wish that is that. Happily for them, "not anything" isn't correct enough. So we press them, and that they often comply with up with some hobby they have deemed boring or boring. We ask them about the hobby – why they are doing it, what precisely is dull about it, and what it includes.

This manner usually includes dragging records out of students, and at the same time as it's a pain for teachers, it's miles important for students. Once they may be secure sharing a sentence or, we ask them to increase. So, as opposed to "I had elegance" as a response, students analyze to mention, "I had dance class, which became really amusing because we're learning a brand new routine to a new tune and I simply love it." when college students can without difficulty shape complete thoughts and have interaction in backward and forward, this is verbal exchange. It takes time, but it's well worth it as it instills students with character.

Forming and fostering relationships

Once children can maintain communication, they can begin to shape relationships. They discover folks that proportion comparable personalities or hobbies, and that they speak approximately them. Students make and lose friends fairly regularly – this is part of growing up and training their social talents. They analyze that being rude or too talkative damages relationships, whilst listening and having something thrilling to contribute improves them. They expand and maintain sturdy relationships with friends, which will become a virtuous cycle of social talent acquisition (and a supply of fun and support).

As soon as college students can form relationships with peers, they emerge as higher at engaging strangers. Their ability to speak with and concentrate to their buddies makes them extra able to making use of these identical competencies with new humans, for this reason enhancing their potential to make new friends and buddies.

Eventually, once human beings are comfy engaging with strangers, they could then apply their social skills to constructing relationships with special forms of human beings in one-of-a-kind settings. The sorts of relationships required in functioning, a successful adult's life are manifold and consist of professional relationships with people who are older, more youthful, in unique departments, and from one-of-a-kind backgrounds. Interpersonal relationships will consist of in most cases friends, however additionally prolonged own family and mentors. Beyond that, having the ability to engage people from specific international locations, of different social or financial backgrounds, or people with one-of-a-kind beliefs and worldviews, opens up the maximum fruitful opportunities and studies. None of that is viable without being able to build and preserve relationships, and relationships are built on appropriate and adept social capabilities.

Legal professional abilities

Three of the most essential social capabilities are being able to provide an explanation for, negotiate, and convince. We name these the "attorney skills" because they are at the center of that profession, but are vital for lots of other kinds of work and reports as well.

First, being capable of explaining a subject to others is deeply crucial. It starts with children explaining themselves after they get in trouble and is an ability everybody ought to cultivate at some point in their lives. It's far the significant ability required of teachers and coaches. Exceptional parents are folks that can explain ideas nicely to their children.

Negotiation abilities

Children examine this primary from their friends; who get to be "it" in tag, how to share, and who's first in line are all examples of youngsters having to appoint negotiation. However, it will become increasingly critical as adults, whilst people must learn to compromise or co-exist with those we disagree with.

Sooner or later, mastering to persuade others of a concept is one of the most difficult, but most beneficial, of social competencies. Kids learn this in convincing their dad and mom handy over greater duty and privilege, but as adults, we use it while we argue or whilst we want to get our way.

Lively listening

There's extra to social abilities than speaking – understanding how to pay attention is enormously important. The general public assumes this comes effortlessly for college students too; instructors educate, students pay attention. However, there's a distinction between sitting quietly and actively listening, taking in, and parsing data. So many humans confuse listening with waiting for the speaker to prevent talking so we can communicate, but these folks have negative social skills.

The primary ability to foster when thinking about listening capabilities is persistence. Occasionally listening is sitting there and hearing what a person has to mention, and giving them the time to say it. Persistence is a beneficial talent on its own and can be a profoundly helpful approach – oftentimes in a dispute or difficult state of affairs, a purchaser or buddy or tremendous different simply desires to "sense heard." but it's also essential to research endurance when listening so that you can rent your attention and empathy.

Attention is the subsequent step of lively listening. Beyond simply listening to what a person has said, you want so one can see it from their attitude, understand what their meaning is (each on and below the surface), and analyze what is being stated. This ability is essential not just in listening, however studying and thinking are preferred.

In the end, having empathy is the mark of a true active listener. Those with empathy understand why someone says what they say and experience how they experience it. This doesn't suggest you have to accept as true with everything a person says, however, it guarantees you absolutely apprehend, and it allows the speaker to admire your listening.

Consider and reliability

Being able to all the above competencies, gaining the considering of others must be fairly easy. Being trustworthy calls for the capacity to pay attention, but also reply usefully, after which also time and again and always.

This is additionally called being "dependable" – whilst a friend is having a difficult time, or when a boss needs an undertaking carried out now, they recognize they are able to anticipate you because you've come via earlier than. Gaining acceptance as true with, even of close buddies, additionally calls for tact and socialization, and because being trustworthy needs to be an aim in and of itself, growing social capabilities are a worthy pursuit.

Self-belief

Self-assurance isn't clearly an ability; it is also the consequence of years of practicing social skills. The maximum confident college students are frequently folks that experience the maximum comfort in their elegance and with their work, and those college students experience relaxed because they don't must suppose so difficult about the way to interact with others – it appears to return evidently to them after so much enjoy.

Nonetheless, confidence is also an ability. Having it instills self-belief in you amongst other people, making socialization even easier. It facilitates set up which you are truthful and successful, that are each useful in terms of the opportunities with a purpose to be open to you, but even further because like trustworthiness, confidence is a worthy purpose itself.

Networking

As a realistic instance of the application of social abilities, we will look at networking. folks who are satisfactory at "networking" are the ones who have the first-class social capabilities – individuals who are the maximum convincing, thrilling to be around, truthful, loquacious, and confident. And it's far regularly genuine that those with the biggest and quality networks are frequently the maximum successful: "someone is someone through other human beings," because the Ubuntu philosophy goes.

At the same time as networking can stumble upon because of the cynical version of friendship, the abilities required to succeed at it are similar to those that power dating improvement in all other regions. People with satisfactory social skills locate exceptional partners, pleasant careers, first-class colleges, and make pleasant friends. And aren't these the entire factor of "achievement" anyway?

Institution lessons, verbal exchange practice, and informal surroundings

One thing human beings often don't realize is that public training is meant to do more than just "make human beings clever." one among its major goals is socialization – faculty is a socializing system supposed to make certain students grow up into residents able to interacting responsibly and effectively with different members of society.

A great deal of social learning comes from genuinely being at faculty and interacting with other students and teachers. This method is in addition enforced at a few education establishments wherein students want to be able to talk and pay attention beyond just writing.

Writing and social talents

Beyond speaking, the writing taught has to require the ability to influence and establish agreement on the part of readers. College students must be asked to try to get their work to be "relatable" so that capacity readers can discover with it, and as a result, higher apprehend and respect the arguments provided.

It is able to be an easy form of persuasive writing in which college students have to be able to form an opinion, articulate their reasoning, and accomplish that in an enticing way. Easy, rote responses are never truly sufficient, so social wondering is significant to the writing system in this layout. Once more, this needs to be required even for our maximum fundamental curriculum — the abilities important for extra advanced essays demand more articulation and reliability.

Writing-as-social skills are on even brighter display at Taipei teen Tribune, the exhibit eBook for our top writers. These college students broaden their personal subjects, talk advanced troubles with coaches, and delve deep into their research and studying for articles. Their work can vary from arguable to candid, and those writers are capable of hire this advanced social thinking in their everyday interactions, making them gregarious and engaged young humans.

Cultural publicity

Many students around the sector best hardly ever engage with humans exclusive from them. Students need to get the risk to fulfill quite a number of schooling professionals from a wealth of backgrounds. College students see distinct personalities and ways of wondering many of their peers do no longer.

Additionally, whilst considering their work, they have the opportunity to question and have interaction with knowledgeable and international minds regarding diverse topics, hence presenting an international angle.

Finally, many faculties make a point of introducing students to the worldwide and Western traditions. in lots of sessions, college students are responsible for reading novels or quick tales, nearly all from the Western literary canon. Writers are further uncovered to more than a few media including music, movie, and popular culture. This background no longer most effective improves their writing variety and skills, it makes them extra confident after they come upon new kinds of human beings from one-of-a-kind backgrounds.

The downfall of one-on-one

As a writing service, every so often we hear from households that don't want to sign up for a class but instead ask for one-on-one tutoring. This but, need to be endorsed if students want to have a look at for a specific check or in training for a presentation, speech, or to help with a massive task.

Certainly one of the largest troubles is that one-on-one is dull. Organization classes are tons extra attractive due to the fact special personalities can come together and interact, even as no unmarried pupil is liable for always engaging the trainer. Students broaden friendships, see their peers also make mistakes, and they recognize they're now not by themselves in struggling with very difficult work. when college students are with a writing instruct one-on-one, however, the scholar has to not handiest do all the classwork, but additionally, the work of usually answering each query the trainer poses, with none of the advantages of accomplishing a category tradition. That is hard on students and until they're capable of form a robust bond with the trainer, they are plenty less likely to revel in the lesson than if they had some classmates.

Another vital motive why one-on-one tutoring is greater complicated than beneficial is that it may, in a few circumstances, teach students that they deserve unique interests separate from the organization. This is what dad and mom are for, now not educational applications or coaching. Students need to discover ways to perform in environments that exist independently of them, not those tailor-made for his or her particular needs. One-on-one tutoring, but, is tailored to a scholar's agenda, stage, and character.

Kids shouldn't analyze they may be unique due to the fact their parents tell them so or due to the fact, mom and dad can have enough money for specialized instructional coaching for them. Kids ought to examine they aren't special until they work tough and increase attributes and competencies that help them really stand out.

Having social competencies vs. not
Even considering how essential social abilities are, the

majority nevertheless lack these skills. Many human beings, adults and kids alike, are awkward, lack self-assurance, and are clumsy in their interactions. And for the general public, this can be okay. Now not each person has to be Tony Stark or Jack Ma. But we've determined that social competencies are essential to achievement in many fields.

Take for instance the story of Robert Oppenheimer vs. Christopher Langan as outlined in Malcolm Gladwell's famous eBook Outliers. Robert Oppenheimer, a man regarded frequently for his mathematical genius but also for his speaking abilities, is lauded as one of the best minds of the 20th century. Chris Langan is a great deal less widely recognized, however possibly at the same highbrow degree as Oppenheimer. However, Langan, from a deprived background, never evolved the extent of socialization Oppenheimer did, and therefore suffered for it.

Social Competence and Social abilities

Is there a distinction between social competence and social abilities? Social competence is the condition of possessing the social, emotional, and highbrow skills and behaviors that had to be triumphant as a member of society. Social skills are the abilities we use to talk and have interaction with each other, each verbally and non-verbally, through gestures, frame language, and our non-public appearance. Both additives are important and useful, permitting a person to have a fixed of capabilities wished for social interaction; but trouble occurring nowadays is the shortage of those talents in special needs students. Students with disabilities have difficulties establishing relationships and/or expressing their emotions. These students can benefit from social competence and social abilities through the creation of green studying surroundings and demonstration of the development of interplay.

Whilst students omit out social possibilities in an ordinary lecture room they're lacking out opportunities for academic enrichment (participating on projects, working in pairs, collaborating in magnificence discussions) as well as personal and social enrichment (making new friends, gambling games). The lengthy-term goals are to preserve building relationships through the years and having extra social competence. "The sooner we are able to intrude with these kids and educate the necessary social talents, the more likely it's far that they will end up adjusted and socially capable teens and adults". Early life is a critical time in society; it is a developmental length where youngsters have an experimental foundation for growing a variety of social abilities. Consequently, if we put in force these capabilities at an early age, these kids can be capable of following them to their everyday lives and communicate with others extra

Specializing in the child social capabilities

What you suspect are the maximum important social abilities in our society, and the way could you begin to teach them to infants and infants? Social behaviors have exceptional degrees. "The primary stage of psychosocial development agrees with". These stages encompass consider autonomy and initiative. Accept as true with is received when a little one feels that every one his or her needs are met. For instance, the mother choices the infant up while it is crying. The mom offers the child meals when it is hungry. The mom modifications the baby's diaper when he or she is dirty. That is how infants turn out to be social. The toddler is able to communicate with the parent through crying. The second level of psychosocial development is autonomy. "Autonomy takes place because the developing toddler reaches the second year and starts to transport around inside the environment". During this level children are capable of attempt matters on their own. As an example, they will try to use their personal potty. Some of the babies are seeking to be more impartial. This means they try to do matters without their mother and father's help. Social abilities are very important for children to learn. Social competencies are needed to participate in society. As we realize, you should be able to speak so that you can be social. Children who work in companies are gaining knowledge of their social abilities and they can work with and cooperate with others. "Research indicates that social abilities and emotional improvement (contemplated in the capacity to pay attention, make transitions from one hobby to every other, and cooperate with others) are a completely crucial part of faculty readiness", the final stage within the social development initiative. At this stage, children are looking for out how to do matters alone

Some other way to promote prosocially is to permit your toddler to want to help differently. as an example, taking your infant to donate gadgets to homeless humans, assist your baby learns that it is right to assist others. You could also be a terrific redecorate for your infant. Children learn from what they see. "Model the conduct you need younger children to collect". Permit's say a person assists you positioned air in your tire. You told the person "thanks" and also you gave them a few dollars. There are unique approaches to help children examine prosocially.

Teaching social capabilities in the lecture room

The reason for this evaluation is to evaluate the effectiveness of the Cool children social competencies application. Fister, Conrad, and Kemp (1998) created this software as a manner to train college students' basic and unique social competencies that could allow them to be triumphant academically as well as socially. Getting into a school social surroundings is an extensive and foundational experience for youngsters. Standard age college students have to efficiently transition from well-hooked up, at easing social interactions with caregivers to explicit and implicit social regulations and interactions in a faculty environment. Being able to efficaciously make this transition with instructors and classmates is regularly key to a hit faculty experience. Early behavior problems in children positioned them at threat for escalating educational troubles which include grade retention and school dropout. Not most effective is a pupil's conduct drastically related to grades, it has additionally been located that insufficient social competencies can boom vulnerability to depression as well as social anxiety. Similarly, one of the more essential findings became the correlation between bad social capabilities, aggression, and violent conduct. Research shows that 10% of early school-age kids entering the instructional system each display prevalence for aggressive conduct issues; for socio-economically disadvantaged youngsters it can be as high as

25%. Research factors to the truth that a valuable and value impact method of interrupting the development of conduct troubles in youngsters is to intervene with social talents education when they're younger and maximum impressionable.

Few studies observed coaching staff and their fidelity to specific social abilities packages. The usage of triangulation in staring at the study room might be a robust development as a manner to now not simplest confirm instructor constancy to the program but to verify reports of changed classroom conduct. The query is, to what quantity is Cool children related to better trainer ratings of social competence and decrease scores of antisocial behavior for simple age students? More than one observer will be an excellent way to answer this query.

Social abilities required for cooperative learning

To recognize the talents necessary to achieve cooperative studying you first need to have a short creation to the subject of cooperative learning itself. Cooperative gaining knowledge of most typically refers to a technique of instruction that organizes college students to work in agencies toward a commonplace aim or outcome, or proportion a common hassle or mission in one of this manner that they can only reach completing the work thru behavior that demonstrates interdependence even as keeping man or woman contributions and efforts responsible. So as for powerful cooperative studying to occur five vital elements are wished; high-quality interdependence, face-to-face interactions, individual duty, social abilities, and organization processing. Social skills being the foundation to achieving all the different factors required, without this set of capabilities the character learner will discover it tough to cooperate with others. Social abilities are paramount to making use of cooperative mastering to instructional duties. Fostering the improvement of social competencies calls for an environment that is conducive to the organization getting to know. An area in which the character learner can locate their personal non-public space, at the same time be related to others in the group. This will take some innovative thinking on behalf of the instructor or venture leader. A reorganization of the gap is every so often vital, deliberating environmental influences including lighting fixtures, sounds, and temperature. When the individual learner's distraction level is saved to a minimum they're capable of have extra participation within the organization. Recognition is also the main force that motivates each man or woman and the group to study.

Chapter Seven

Social Learning, Cognition and Personal Development

Social getting to know theories advocate that youngsters learn to showcase competitive behaviors due to the fact they observe others performing aggressively and might see how these behaviors are bolstered over the years. Social studying theories emphasize the significance of the social context and posit that individuals can analyze by way of watching others' actions and whether those people are definitely or negatively strengthened while showing competitive behaviors. Studies by way of Bandura have also cautioned that young kids imitate adults' aggressive moves that they witness in contrived social settings. As a consequence, aggressive behavior is a concept to arise as it has been both modeled and bolstered through the years.

Social gaining knowledge of principle views the course of human development in terms of kid's socialization reports and acquisition of self-law. Kid's development of personality traits, such as dependency and aggression, as well as their talent in academics, sports activities, arts, or professions are assumed to emerge from learning reviews embedded in the social milieu of their own family, peers, gender, and way of life. The social mastering concept defines children's socialization in phrases of specific social learning reviews, including modeling, tuition, and reinforcement, and the cognitions, emotions, and behavior that emerge from these formative reviews. Kid's private reactions have been explained historically using persona constructs, inclusive of identity, conditioning, or pressure reduction, however are defined contemporaneously in cognitive terms, consisting of self-efficacy beliefs and various self-regulatory tactics. Self-law is essential to a kid's development due to the fact socialization includes giving up without delay enjoyable activities or acquainted techniques of coping to reap not on time advantages. A key supply of motivation underlying kid's self-regulatory improvement is their notion of self-efficacy. There is evidence that psychosocial impacts of households and peers, consisting of parental dreams and peer pressures, have an effect on kid's self-efficacy ideals, aspirations, and stages of self-law. Kid's self-regulatory processes and beliefs, in turn, causally affect their emotional, moral, and educational development.

This concept affords the idea of how social norms are learned and internalized throughout early life. Although this principle was at first advanced to describe the illegal activity and deviant conduct, its propositions also can be carried out to high-quality social getting to know. Akers and associates identified four core constructs of social gaining knowledge of differential association, differential reinforcement, imitation or modeling, and definitions. Differential association refers back to the direct affiliation with agencies that specific certain norms, values, and attitudes. The businesses with whom one is related provide the social context in which all social learning occurs. The most vital agencies include own family and pals, however also can include greater secondary sources consisting of the media. In step with Sutherland's differential affiliation theory, studying takes place in step with the frequency, period, priority, and depth of youth' social interactions. kids will research from and internalize social norms if (1) associations arise in advance in improvement (priority), (2) they associate frequently with others who engage within the behavior (frequency), (three) interactions occur over an extended time frame (period), and (4) interactions involve people with whom one is near (e.g., friends and family) as opposed to greater casual or superficial interactions (depth). The greater one's styles of differential affiliation are balanced closer to publicity to prosocial, high-quality conduct and attitudes, the greater the possibility that one can even have interaction in nice behaviors. Affiliation with companies affords the social context in which publicity to differential reinforcement, imitation of fashions, and definitions for behaviors take vicinity.

Differential reinforcement refers to the stability of past, gift, and predicted destiny rewards and punishments for given behavior which includes the reactions and sanctions of all important social companies, in particular those of friends and family, but also can consist of other businesses which include colleges and churches. Particularly, behaviors are reinforced thru rewards (i.e., effective reinforcement, e.g., peer acceptance of behaviors) and avoidance of punishments (i.e., terrible reinforcement, e.g., peer rejection of behaviors) or weakened although receiving punishments (i.e., high-quality punishment; e.g., being grounded via mother and father) and loss of rewards (i.e., a terrible punishment, e.g., having the family automobile taken away. Behaviors that are reinforced, both thru social rewards and thru the avoidance of social punishments, are much more likely to be repeated, while behaviors that elicit social punishments are much less possibly to be repeated. Consequently, thru differential reinforcement, individuals are conditioned to internalize the social norms which might be valued by way of the organization.

Social behavior is likewise fashioned by means of imitating or modeling others' conduct. Individuals examine behaviors by looking at those around them, mainly near others including mother and father, siblings, or friends. The importance of social gaining knowledge of and imitation mainly is strengthened the extra similar the individuals are. The social effect has an effect on youth while teenagers are exposed to the behaviors and norms of others (i.e., mere exposure) and examine the advantageous consequences others acquire from such behaviors (i.e., vicarious studying). Adolescents then internalize such social norms and model the behaviors in destiny times.

in the end, definitions are the attitudes, rationalizations, or meanings that one attaches to a given behavior that defines the conduct as suitable or horrific, right or wrong, justified or unjustified, and suitable or inappropriate. The greater individuals have learned that particular attitudes or behaviors are true or applicable (fine definition) or as justified (neutralizing definition) in preference to as undesirable (terrible definition), the much more likely they're to have interaction within the behaviors. Those definitions are learned thru imitation and next differential reinforcement by using participants in their peer and family agencies. even though there can be norm warfare in phrases of the definitions promoted by using one's peers (e.g., the high-quality definition for alcohol) and dad and mom (e.g., the negative definition for alcohol), the relative weight of such definitions will determine whether a teenager endorses the social norm and engages in the conduct. A person will engage inside the behavior whilst the superb and neutralizing definitions of the behavior offset the terrible definitions.

The social getting to know theorists found that the complexity of human conduct can't without difficulty be explained by means of conventional behavioral theories. Bandura diagnosed that human beings learn the first-rate deal from watching other humans and seeing the rewards and/or punishments that other human beings receive. Social mastering theorists do not deny they have an effect on reinforcement and punishment, but instead, they suggest that it is able to be experienced thru commentary and does now not require direct, private experience as Skinner could argue. In addition, observational learning requires cognition, something that radical behaviorists don't forget out of doors the realm of mental studies, given that cognition can't be found. Bandura took a broad theoretical perspective on social mastering, whereas Rotter and Mischel focused extra intently on particular cognitive elements of social learning and behavior.

It's also critical to point out an artificial distinction that is hard to avoid within the chapters of this section. Chapters ten, eleven, and twelve are roughly installation as chapters on radical behaviorism and formal getting to know the idea, observed by way of social getting to know, after which concluding with cognitive theories on personality development. But, as may be evident, the chapters overlap an outstanding deal. For example, Dollard and Miller's attempt to discover a center ground between Freud and Skinner brought about their initial descriptions of social learning, which supplied a prelude to this bankruptcy. Bandura, Rotter, and Mischel deal with a number of components of cognition in their theories, but they may be now not as absolutely centered on cognition as are Kelly, Beck, and Ellis, for this reason, the separation of this chapter from the following one. In the Social studying concept, Bandura had this to mention:

A valid criticism of intense behaviorism is that, in a lively attempt to keep away from spurious internal causes, it has unnoticed determinants of behavior bobbing up from cognitive functioning. due to the fact, some of the inner reasons invoked by using theorists through the years have been sick-based does no longer justify with the exception of all internal determinants from medical inquiry such as research screen that people analyze and keep behaviors plenty better via the use of cognitive aids that they generate than with the aid of strengthened repetitive performance...A idea that denies that thoughts can alter moves does now not lend itself with ease to the explanation of complicated human behaviors.

Albert Bandura and social mastering theory

Bandura is the most widely identified man or woman inside the area of social learning principle, notwithstanding the data that Dollard and Miller hooked up the sphere and Rotter turned into starting to observe cognitive social studying some years earlier than Bandura. Though Bandura's research has had the most substantial effect, and the results of modeling on competitive behavior remain studied nowadays (see "persona idea in actual existence" at the end of the bankruptcy). Therefore, we can begin this chapter by examining the basics of Bandura's social mastering perspective.

Quick Biography of Albert Bandura

Albert Bandura turned into born in 1925, inside the small metropolis of Mundare, in northern Alberta, Canada. His mother and father had emigrated from Jap Europe (his father from Poland, his mom from Ukraine), and finally stored enough money to shop for a farm. Farming in northern Canada become now not clean. certainly one of Bandura's sisters died for the duration of a flu pandemic, certainly one of his brothers died in a hunting accident, and a part of the own family farm was lost in the course of the first-rate melancholy. Despite the fact that the Bandura family endured, and maintained an active and satisfying home.

Even though Bandura's parents lacked any formal schooling, they stressed its cost. no matter having handiest one small school in the town, which lacked each instructor and academic sources, the city's youngsters advanced love of studying and most of them attended universities around the sector. Following the encouragement of his dad and mom, Bandura also sought a huge form of different stories whilst he was young. He worked in a fixtures manufacturing plant, and done preservation on the Trans-Alaska toll road. The latter revel in, especially, added Bandura to a ramification of uncommon people and offered a completely unique angle on psychopathology in normal existence.

While Bandura went to the University of British Columbia, he meant to fundamental in biology. However, he had joined a carpool with engineering and pre-med college students who attended instructions early in the morning. Bandura looked for a category to shape this timetable and came about to word that an introductory psychology direction was presented at that time. Bandura loved the class so much that he changed his primary to psychology, receiving his bachelor's diploma in 1949. Bandura then attended graduate school at the college of Iowa, in a psychology department strongly inspired by using Kenneth Spence, a former student of Clark Hull. For this reason, the psychology application at the University of Iowa became strongly behavioral in its orientation, and they had been well versed inside the behavioral studies carried out in the psychology branch at Yale University.

As we noticed inside the preceding bankruptcy, John Dollard and Neal Miller had set up the sphere of social learning at Yale inside the 1930s, but that they had performed so within the conceptual pointers of Hullian getting to know principle. Bandura became no longer especially inquisitive about Hull's approach to gaining knowledge of, however, he becomes impressed by Dollard and Miller's ideas of modeling and imitation. Bandura acquired his Ph.D. in clinical psychology in 1952, after which started out a postdoctoral position at the Wichita steerage center. Bandura turned into drawn to this function, in part, because the psychologist in charge became no longer closely immersed in the Freudian psychodynamic method that changed into nevertheless so popular in scientific psychology.

Following his postdoctoral training, Bandura became a member of the college at Stanford College, in which he spent the relaxation of his career. The chairman of Bandura's branch was analyzing frustration and aggression, and this inspired Bandura to start his own research on social learning and aggression. These studies discovered the important position that modeling performs in social learning and soon resulted in the eBook of Adolescent Aggression (co-authored by Richard Walters, Bandura's first graduate scholar; Bandura & Walters, 1959). This line of research also caused the well-known "Bobo" doll research, which helped to demonstrate that even younger kids can research competitive behavior via staring at fashions. Bandura then became inquisitive about self-regulatory behavior in kids, and one of the colleagues he collaborated with was Walter Mischel, whose work we are able to cope with later in this bankruptcy. at some point in his long and efficient profession, Bandura has become an increasing number of inquisitive about the position played by way of cognition in social gaining knowledge of, finally renaming his concept to mirror his social cognitive angle on human mastering. He also examined the position of the man or woman in influencing the nature of the environment in which they enjoy existence, and the way their very own expectations of self-efficacy affect their willingness to take part in aspects of that life.

Bandura has obtained several honors in the course of his career. Included among them, he has served as president of the American mental affiliation and received a distinguished medical Contribution Award from APA. He acquired the William James Award from the American Psychological Society (known these days as the association for psychological science), a Guggenheim Fellowship, the distinguished Contribution Award from the worldwide Society for research in Aggression, and a distinguished Scientist Award from the Society of Behavioral remedy.

Bandura has additionally been elected to the yank Academy of Arts and Sciences, to the Institute of medication of the countrywide Academy of Sciences, and he has obtained several honorary degrees from universities around the sector. The list is going on, no longer the least of that's his wonderful Lifetime Contribution to Psychology Award, received from APA in 2004.

Bandura social getting to know idea of establishes its independence

Despite the fact that social learning concept has its foundation within the work of Dollard and Miller, they addressed social getting to know within the context of Hullian mastering concept (complete with mathematical formulae). Bandura shifted the point of interest of social studying far from traditional behavioral views, and established social getting to know as an idea on its very own. Bandura also freely mentioned cognition in the getting to know procedure, something that in advance behaviorists had actively prevented. With the aid of acknowledging each the external techniques of reinforcement and punishment and the inner cognitive tactics that make humans so complicated, Bandura supplied a comprehensive theory of persona that has been very influential.

Even though Bandura criticized each operant conditioning and Pavlovian conditioning as being too radical, he depended on a process that came from Pavlovian conditioning studies for one among his most influential concepts: using modeling. The modeling system turned into developed by Mary cowl Jones, a student of John B.

Watson, in her tries to counter-situation found out phobias. Next to the infamous "Little Albert" studies conducted through Watson, Jones used fashions to interact in a pleasant way with a rabbit that check subjects were conditioned to worry. After a few periods, the test subjects had been now not afraid of the rabbit. This could have been the first use of conduct therapy, and Bandura's use of the procedure helped to carry collectively unique behavioral disciplines.

Possibly one in all Bandura's most significant contributions, however, has been the software of his theory to many styles of media. Congressional committees have debated the impact of modeling aggression thru violent television packages, films, and video games. We now have rankings on each of these styles of media, and but the controversy continues due to the tiers of aggression seen in our schools, specially, and society in widespread. Bandura's Bobo doll studies are truely amongst of the great known studies in psychology, and they are also the various most influential in terms of realistic each day packages. The long list of awards that Bandura has acquired is a testimony to each his influence on psychology and the honor that have an effect on has earned for him.

Reciprocal Determinism

One of the maximum vital elements of Bandura's view on how persona is learned is that each one of us is an agent of alternate, absolutely collaborating in our environment and influencing the environmental contingencies that behaviorists accept as true with have an effect on our behavior. Those interactions can be considered three unique ways. The first is to recollect behavior as a characteristic of the person and the surroundings. On this view, personal tendencies (or traits) and the consequences of our movements (reinforcement or punishment) integrate to reason our conduct. This angle is closest to the radical behaviorism of Skinner. The second one view considers that non-public tendencies and the surroundings have interaction, and the end result of the interaction reasons our behavior, a view fairly closer to that of Dollard and Miller. In each of these views, behavior is caused, or determined, through dispositional and environmental factors, the conduct itself isn't a component in how that behavior comes about. however, consistent with Bandura, social learning principle emphasizes that behavior, non-public elements, and environmental factors are all equal, interlocking determinants of each other. This idea is referred to as reciprocal determinism.

Early theories considered behavior to be a feature of the character and their surroundings, or a function of the interaction between the person and their environment. Bandura believed that behavior itself influences each the character and the surroundings, every of which in turn affects behavior and every different. The end result is a complicated interaction of things referred to as reciprocal determinism.

Reciprocal determinism can be visible in everyday observations, which include those made by using Bandura and others throughout their research of aggression. As an example, about seventy five percent of the time, adverse conduct outcomes in unfriendly responses, while pleasant acts seldom results in such results. With little attempt, it becomes smooth to understand individuals who create bad social climates. Accordingly, whilst it may nevertheless be authentic that changing environmental contingencies modifications conduct, it's also real that converting conduct alters the environmental contingencies. This effects in a completely unique perspective on freedom vs. determinism. Generally we think about determinism as something that eliminates or restricts our freedom. However, Bandura believed that individuals can deliberately act as agents of change within their environment, thus altering the elements that determine their behavior. In different words, we've the freedom to steer that which determines our conduct:

Given the same environmental constraints, individuals who've many behavioral options and are adept at regulating their very own conduct will enjoy greater freedom than will individuals whose personal resources are restrained.

Observational mastering and aggression

Social mastering is likewise generally known as observational gaining knowledge of, because it comes about because of watching models. Bandura became inquisitive about social components of gaining knowledge of at the start of his profession. Skilled as a clinical psychologist, he started out working with juvenile delinquents, an extremely old term that is basically a socio-felony description of youth who engage in antisocial conduct. Within the 1950s there was already studies on the relationships between competitive boys and their mother and father, in addition to some theoretical views regarding the effects of different toddler-rearing practices on the conduct and attitudes of adolescent boys. A great deal of the research focused, however, on sociological issues concerned inside the environment of antisocial boys. Deciding on a distinct technique, Bandura decided to look at boys who had no apparent sociological risks (inclusive of poverty, language difficulties due to current immigration, low IQ, and so forth.). Bandura and Walters confined their pattern to boys of common or above common intelligence, from intact houses, with step by step hired parents, whose families were settled in the USA for at the least three generations. No kids from minority companies were included both. In different words, the men were from reputedly traditional, White, center-magnificence American households. And yet, half of the boys studied had been recognized through the county probation provider or their faculty steerage center as demonstrating serious, repetitive, antisocial, competitive behaviours.

Bringing up the work of Dollard and Miller, in addition to others who paved the way for social learning theory, Bandura and Walters commenced their observe on adolescent aggression through inspecting how the parents of delinquents educate their children to be socialized. Working from a preferred getting to know perspective, emphasizing cues and results, they located massive issues in the improvement of socialization a few of the antisocial boys. These boys evolved dependency, a necessary step closer to socialization, but they were not taught to comply their conduct with the expectations of society. Consequently, they started to demand instant and unconditional gratification from their surroundings, something that seldom occurs. Of direction, this failure to study proper socialization does no longer necessarily cause aggression, due to the fact that it may additionally cause lifestyles including the hobo, the bohemian, or the "beatnik". Why then perform a little boys come to be so aggressive? To in brief summarize their observation, Bandura and Walters found that dad and mom of delinquent boys have been much more likely to version competitive conduct and to use coercive punishment (instead of reasoning with their children to assist them comply with social norms). Despite the fact that parental modeling of competitive behavior teaches such behavior to kids, those parents have a tendency to be effective at suppressing their kids' competitive behavior at home. In evaluation, however, they provide diffused encouragement for aggression outside the home. As an end result, those poorly socialized boys are in all likelihood to displace the aggressive impulses that increase in the domestic, and they're nicely educated in doing so. in the event that they to associate with a antisocial institution (inclusive of a gang), they're furnished with an opportunity to learn new and more powerful methods to engage in antisocial behaviour, and they may be without delay rewarded for undertaking such behaviours.

Having discovered evidence that mother and father of competitive, delinquent boys had modeled competitive conduct, Bandura and his colleagues embarked on a series of research on the modeling of aggression. To start with, children were given the opportunity to play in a room containing a selection of toys, including the five-foot tall, inflated Bobo doll (a toy clown). As part of the test, a grownup (the version) become also invited into the room to join in the sport. When the version exhibited clean competitive conduct toward the Bobo doll, and then the kids were allowed to play on their very own, they kids verified competitive behavior as nicely. The children, who observed a version that was no longer competitive, seldom confirmed competitive behavior, accordingly confirming that the aggression in the experimental group resulted from observational mastering. in the second study, children who found the behavior of competitive models on film additionally validated a significant boom in competitive behavior, suggesting that the physical presence of the model is not necessary (providing an important implication for violent aggression on TV and in films; see "character in principle in actual life" at the give up of the bankruptcy). in addition to confirming the role of commentary or social learning in the improvement of competitive conduct, those studies also supplied a starting point for examining what it's far that makes a version influential.

One of the big findings in this line of research on aggression is the influence of models on behavioral restraint. Whilst kids are uncovered to models who aren't competitive and who inhibit their personal behavior, the kids additionally tend to inhibit their very own aggressive responses and to limit their variety of behavior in popular. For this reason, kids can analyze from others, particularly their parents, a way to regulate their conduct in socially suitable approaches. When the inappropriate conduct of others is punished, the children looking at also are vicariously punished, and probable to enjoy tension, if now not outright fear, once they take into account conducting similar beside the point conduct. However, whilst models behave aggressively and their behavior is rewarded, or even simply tolerated, the kid's personal tendency to restrict competitive impulses can be weakened. This weakening of restraint that could then result in appearing out competitive impulses is referred to as disinhibition:

Modeling might also produce disinhibitory outcomes in several ways. Whilst people reply approvingly or even indifferently to the moves of assailants, they create the impact that aggression is not simplest applicable however expected in comparable conditions. Through thus legitimizing aggressive conduct, observers anticipate much less risk of reprimand or loss of self-recognize for such action.

Traits of the modeling state of affairs

While one character matches the behavior of some other, there are numerous views on why that matching conduct takes place. Theorists who advise that matching conduct effects from easy imitation don't permit for any significant mental changes. Dollard and Miller discussed imitation of their attempts to combine conventional gaining knowledge of theory with a psychodynamic angle, however they did not enhance the theory very far. A more conventional psychodynamic technique describes matching behavior because the end result of identity, the idea that an observer connects with a version in a few psychological manner. However, identification way different things to special theorists, and the time period stays really vague. In social gaining knowledge of, as it has been advanced by Bandura, modeling is the term that fine describes and, therefore, is used to symbolize the psychological procedures that underlie matching behaviours.

Observational learning thru modeling isn't always merely an alternative to Pavlovian or operant conditioning: gaining knowledge of could be particularly hard, no longer to say hazardous, if people had to rely totally at the effects of their own movements to inform them what to do. fortuitously, most human conduct is discovered observationally through modeling: from observing others one bureaucracy an concept of ways new behaviors are achieved, and on later occasions this coded facts serves as a manual for motion.

Individuals fluctuate in the diploma to which they can be inspired by means of models, and no longer all fashions are similarly effective. According to Bandura, three elements are maximum influential in phrases of the effectiveness of modeling conditions: the traits of the model, the attributes of the observers, and the outcomes of the model's actions. The most relevant traits of an influential version are excessive reputation, competence, and power. When observers are unsure about a situation, they rely upon cues to indicate what they perceive as proof of beyond fulfillment with the aid of the version. Such cues include standard appearance, symbols of socioeconomic fulfillment (e.g., a flowery sports vehicle), and signs of expertise (e.g., a health practitioner's lab coat). Given that those models appear to be successful themselves, it appears logical that observers might need to imitate their behavior. Folks that are low in self-esteem, established, and who lack self-assurance aren't necessarily much more likely to be motivated by using models. Bandura proposed that when modeling is used to explicitly broaden new abilities, the ones who will advantage maximum from the situation are individuals who are greater talented and greater venturesome.

Notwithstanding the capacity influence of fashions, the whole procedure of observational getting to know in a social getting to know surroundings might likely no longer be successful if not for 4 critical thing processes: attentional procedures, retention processes, production (or replica) processes, and motivational processes. The truth that an observer have to pay attention to a version may seem apparent, but some fashions are much more likely to attract attention. People are more likely to be aware of fashions with whom they partner, although the affiliation is extra cognitive than personal. It is also famous that human beings, who're trendy, inclusive of people who are physically appealing or famous athletes, make for interest-getting fashions. There also are positive forms of media which can be superb at getting people's interest, including tv classified ads. it's far a curious cultural phenomenon that the tv advertisements supplied throughout the countrywide football League's high-quality Bowl have end up almost as lots of the pleasure as the sport itself (or even more thrilling for folks that are not soccer lovers)!

The retention procedures contain in the main an observer's reminiscence for the modeled behavior. The maximum crucial reminiscence approaches, in line with Bandura, are visual imagery and verbal coding, with visual imagery being specifically important early in improvement when verbal abilities are restrained. As soon as modeled behavior has been converted into visual and/or verbal codes, these memories can serve to manual the performance of the conduct at appropriate instances. While the modeled conduct is produced through the observer, the so-referred to as manufacturing process, the re-enactment can be broken down into the cognitive organization of the responses, their initiation, next monitoring, and subsequently the refinement of the conduct based totally on informative feedback. Producing complicated modeled behaviors is not constantly a clean mission:

A not unusual hassle in mastering complex capabilities, along with golf or swimming, is that performers can't completely study their responses, and must therefore depend on indistinct kinesthetic cues or verbal reports of onlookers. It is difficult to manual movements which might be most effective in part observable or to identify the corrections needed to obtain a close match between representation and performance.

In the end, motivational strategies determine whether the observer is willing to suit the modeled conduct inside the first area. People are maximum probable to model behaviors that result in a final results they value, and if the behavior appears to be powerful for the models who proven the conduct. Given the complexity of the relationships among fashions, observers, the perceived effectiveness of modeled behavior, and the subjective fee of rewards, even the use of distinguished models does now not guarantee that they'll be able to create comparable conduct in observers.

Producing complex behaviours that cannot be without difficulty determined by using the performer can show quite tough. John reduce at the back of the defender to pressure the ball with his knee over the goalie's head and into the goal (above). Samuel rankings a spherical kick in a Taekwondo tournament (proper).

A not unusual false impression concerning modeling is that it simplest leads to gaining knowledge of the behaviors which have been modeled. However, modeling can cause innovative behavior styles. Observers normally see a given conduct performed by using more than one fashions; even in early life one regularly gets to peer each dad and mom version a given conduct. Whilst the conduct is then matched, the observer will normally choose factors from the distinctive fashions, relying on simplest positive aspects of the behavior achieved by means of each, after which create a completely unique pattern that accomplishes the very last behavior. Thus, partial departures from the firstly modeled conduct may be a supply of recent instructions, in particular in innovative endeavors (inclusive of composing music or growing a sculpture). In comparison, but, whilst simple exercises prove useful, modeling can virtually stifle innovation. So, the maximum innovative people appear to be the ones who have been exposed to revolutionary fashions, provided that the fashions aren't so modern as to create an unreasonably tough assignment in modeling their creativity and innovation.

Connections throughout cultures

Although we are constantly surrounded through modeling conditions, the maximum obvious and intentional use of models and modelling is in advertising; as our international becomes an increasing number of international, using commercials that work nicely in a single region may be totally irrelevant in a distinct subculture. Marieke de Mooij, the president of a pass-cultural communications consulting firm in the Netherlands, and a travelling professor at universities inside the Netherlands, Spain, Finland, and Germany, has undertaken the challenging venture of reading how tradition impacts consumer conduct and the effects of those outcomes for advertising and advertising in exclusive societies round the arena.

To a few, increasing globalization suggests that markets around the arena becomes extra much like one another. However, contends that as exclusive cultures become more similar in monetary phrases, their extra private cultural differences will surely end up more good sized! for that reason, it's far vital for worldwide corporations to recognize those cultural variations, in order that marketing and advertising may be correctly adjusted. The project is in spotting and managing the "international-nearby paradox." people in enterprise are taught to think global, however act nearby. This is due to the fact the general public for the duration of the world have a tendency to choose matters that are familiar. They will adopt and enjoy worldwide merchandise, however they remain actual to their very own subculture. as a result, it's miles critical to understand nearby way of life and patron conduct in standard before beginning an advertising campaign in a foreign country.

In her research on way of life and customer behavior, de Mooij (2004b, 2005) addresses a huge kind of subjects, which includes several which can be blanketed in this chapter. In phrases of the characteristics of fashions, many countries do now not emphasize physical splendor and/or stylish garments the way we do in the United States. But, the general aesthetic enchantment of advertising can be more essential in lots of Asian markets, specializing in alternatives for values along with nature and harmony. Given that the us is normally an individualistic culture and maximum Asian cultures are collectivistic, it should be no surprise that individuals tend to recognition on the appeal of the version whereas Asians generally tend to recognition at the enchantment of the general scene and relationships among the diverse aspects depicted within it. In a similar manner, cultures differ in terms of their widespread perspective on locus of control. In cultures that have a tendency to believe that their lives are determined through external forces, the moral authorities (which include the church and the press) are typically depended on. People in such cultures might not be responsiveness to classified ads that call for man or woman restraint, along with efforts to lessen cigarette smoking for higher fitness, due to the fact that they rely on their medical doctors (external sellers) to attend to their fitness.

There also are big differences in how human beings in unique cultures suppose and system statistics, and cognitive procedures underlie all aspects of social studying. Involvement principle shows variations in how individuals and cultures differ of their approach to purchasing, and how advertising must take those differences under consideration. As an instance, among American clients considering a "excessive involvement" product (such as a car), folks that are possibly to buy something respond to advertising in which they study something, broaden a positive mindset closer to the product, after which purchase it (research-feel-do). For normal products, which can be taken into consideration "low involvement," customers respond to marketing in which they learn something, then purchase the product, and perhaps later on they tend to decide upon that logo (research-do-experience). There is now proof that during normally more collectivist cultures which includes Japan, China, and Korea, it is important to first set up a courting between the employer and the customer. Simplest then does the customer buy the particular product, after which they turn out to be extra acquainted with it (feel-do-analyze). For that reason, the very purpose of marketing adjustments from way of life to culture. Evidently, a number of different approaches to advertising exist, based totally on principles which include: persuasion, consciousness, emotions, and likeability. Each of these techniques is based on a extraordinary mental approach, thinking of the observers that the advertiser hopes to steer (the so-called target demographic).

One of the maximum critical elements of advertising, while it's miles being carried from one subculture to some other, is the translation of verbal and written facts. Distinct languages have unique symbolic references. They depend on special myths, records, humor, and art, and failing to tap into such variations is likely to result in bland advertising and marketing that does not appeal to the nearby audience. Different languages are absolutely established differently as properly, possibly requiring which means in a name, and this occasionally makes direct translation impossible. Therefore, an global advertiser have to pick out a distinct name for their product. For example, Coca-Cola is advertised in China because the homonym kekou kele, because of this "tasty and happy". Visual references additionally have cultural meanings. A Nokia ad, proven in Finland, used a squirrel in a woodland to represent properly reception and loose movement in a deep forest. A Chinese group, but, understood it as depicting an animal that lives a long way far from human beings. They actually did no longer understand the reason of the economic. Research on interpersonal verbal exchange patterns indicates that sure nations can be grouped into preferred patterns. primarily based on a assessment of more than one dimensions of preferred verbal style, a number of the countries that share comparable patterns are: 1) the USA, the United Kingdom, Norway, the Netherlands, Sweden, and Denmark; 2) Austria, Finland, and Germany; three) India, China, and Singapore; and 4) Italy, Spain, Belgium, France, Argentina, Brazil, and the Arab global.

As tough as it would appear to cope with these problems (and the many greater we've got now not protected), it is critical for individuals concerned in global advertising and advertising: The cultural kind of nations international as well as in Europe implies that success in one USA does now not routinely suggest fulfillment in other nations…locating the most relevant cultural values is hard, particularly because many researchers are based in Western societies that are individualistic and feature universalistic values. Western marketers, advertisers, and researchers are willing to look for similarities, whereas information the variations could be greater worthwhile…There are global merchandise and international brands, but there are not any international buying motives for such manufacturers because humans aren't worldwide. Understanding human beings throughout cultures is the primary and maximum important step in international advertising and marketing.

Finally, none of these approaches to global advertising and advertising and marketing is going to achieve success if enterprise relationships aren't set up within the first vicinity. Inside the Cultural measurement of worldwide enterprise, Ferraro (2006b) gives a complete guide to know-how cultural variations. In addition to the significance of being aware of such factors, which the very lifestyles of the books and articles on this section belies, Ferraro emphasizes cultural differences in communication. For people operating in a foreign country in which English is not the first language, precise verbal exchange turns into a counted of intent:

Because conversation is so vitally important for undertaking commercial enterprise at home, it ought to come as no surprise that it is similarly important for a hit commercial enterprise overseas. The single first-class manner to come to be an powerful communicator as an expatriate is to analyze the local language. Except knowing how to talk any other language; expatriate candidates should show a willingness to apply it. For a selection of motives, some human beings lack the motivation, confidence, or willingness to throw themselves into conversational situations. [Authors word: see the segment on self-efficacy beneath] ...consequently, communication abilities ought to be assessed in terms of language competency, motivation to learn some other language, and willingness to apply it in professional and personal situations.

Self-regulation and self-efficacy

Self-regulation and self-efficacy are two factors of Bandura's idea that depend closely on cognitive strategies. They represent a character's capacity to control their behavior through inner reward or punishment, in the case of self-regulation, and their beliefs of their ability to obtain favored dreams due to their own moves, inside the case of self-efficacy. Bandura in no way rejects the impact of outside rewards or punishments, however he proposes that such as internal, self-reinforcement and self-punishment expands the capacity for getting to know:

Theories that designate human behavior as solely the manufactured from external rewards and punishments gift a truncated photograph of humans because they own self-reactive capacities that allow them to exercise a few manage over their own emotions, thoughts, and moves. Behavior is consequently regulated with the aid of the interplay of self-generated and outside sources of influence.

Self-law is a general term that consists of each self-reinforcement and self-punishment. Self-reinforcement works basically through its motivational outcomes. Whilst an individual sets a preferred of overall performance for themselves, they judge their behavior and determine whether or no longer has it met the self-determined criteria for praise. Seeing that many sports do no longer have absolute measures of success, the character regularly sets their standards in relative ways. For example, a weight-lifter may maintain track of ways much general weight they raise in every schooling consultation, and then monitor their improvement over the years or as each competition arrives. Although competitions offer the ability for outside praise, the person might nevertheless set a private general for success, together with being glad simplest in the event that they win at least one of the individual lifts. The standards that a man or woman units for themselves can be found out via modeling. This may create problems whilst fashions are surprisingly in a position, lots extra so than the observer is capable of acting (inclusive of getting to know the requirements of a global-magnificence athlete). Kids, but, appear to be greater inclined to model the requirements of low-reaching or fairly in a position fashions, setting standards which are reasonably within their personal attain. In line with Bandura, the cumulative impact of putting requirements and regulating one's very own overall performance in terms of those requirements can result in judgments about one's self. Within a social learning context, bad self-concepts arise while one is susceptible to devalue oneself, whereas tremendous self-concepts get up from a tendency to choose oneself favorably. Typical, the complexity of this method makes predicting the conduct of a man or woman as a substitute hard, and conduct frequently deviates from social norms in methods that would no longer ordinarily be anticipated. However, this appears to be the case in a variety of cultures, suggesting that it is certainly a natural manner for human beings.

As stated above, "perceived self-efficacy refers to ideals in one's abilities to prepare and execute the guides of movement required to produce given attainments". The desire to govern our instances in lifestyles appears to have been with us all through records. In historic instances, while people knew little approximately the arena, they prayed in the hope that benevolent gods could help them and/or shield them from evil gods. Intricate rituals had been developed inside the wish or belief that the gods might reply to their efforts and dedication. As we learned more about our global and the way it works, we additionally discovered that we can have a great impact on it. Most significantly, we can have a direct impact on our immediate non-public surroundings, especially with reference to non-public relationships. What motivates us to strive influencing our environment is specific methods is the belief that we can, certainly, make a distinction in a course we want. Consequently, studies has focused in large part on what people reflect on consideration on their efficacy, in place of on their real ability to attain their dreams.

Self-efficacy has been a popular subject matter for research, and Bandura's e-book Self-Efficacy. We are able to address key troubles in this fascinating topic: the relationships among (1) efficacy ideals and final results expectancies and (2) self-efficacy and shallowness. In any state of affairs, one has ideals approximately one's capacity to influence the state of affairs, and but those ideals are typically balanced in opposition to sensible expectations that change can arise. Each facet of the equation can have each bad and advantageous qualities. Assume, as a pupil, you are worried approximately the rising price of a university education, and also you would really like to task the ones rising charges. You may consider that there's nothing you can do (negative) and training and expenses will inevitably growth (terrible). This twin poor perspective ends in resignation and apathy, really not a favorable scenario. However what if you accept as true with you can alternate the university's route (wonderful), and that the college can reduce sure costs with a view to offset the want for higher tuition (nice). Now you're possibly to have interaction the university network in effective discussions, and this can lead to personal pride (Bandura, 1997). Within the first state of affairs, you aren't possibly to do something, inside the second situation you may maximum likely be relatively motivated to behave, even energized as you work toward efficient modifications. Of route, there are two different possible situations. You may agree with there is not anything you may do (terrible), however that exchange is feasible (wonderful). In this example, you're possibly to devalue yourself, perhaps feeling depressed approximately your own incapacity to perform true. Conversely, you can believe there may be something you could do (advantageous), however that outside forces will make trade difficult or impossible (terrible). This could lead some human beings to task the device regardless of their lack of predicted trade, resulting in protests and other styles of social activism. since all of those situations are based totally on beliefs and expectations, now not on the unknown eventual outcome in an effort to arise, it turns into clear that what we think about our potential to carry out in various conditions, in addition to our real expectancies of the outcomes of those actions, has both complex and profound results on our motivation to interact in a particular behavior or path of motion.

As for self-efficacy and vanity, those terms are often used interchangeably, and on the floor that could seem appropriate. Wouldn't we feel good approximately ourselves if we believed in our talents to acquire our dreams? In fact, self-efficacy and shallowness are entirely distinctive:

There is no fixed dating among ideals approximately one's capabilities and whether or not one likes or dislikes oneself. Individuals might also judge themselves hopelessly inefficacious in a given hobby without suffering any loss of vanity whatsoever, due to the fact they do not invest their self-worth in that pastime.

As an example, my circle of relatives became lively inside

the Korean martial artwork Taekwondo. Taekwondo emphasizes effective kicks. Because I suffer from degenerative joint ailment in both hips, there are positive kicks I surely can't do, and that i don't do any of the kicks especially nicely. But I take delivery of that, and consciousness my interest on areas where i am a success, such as bureaucracy and assisting to teach the white belt magnificence. Likewise, Bandura notes that his complete inefficacy in ballroom dancing does now not lead him into bouts of self-devaluation. So, though it may improve our self-esteem to have sensible emotions of self-efficacy in challenging conditions, there is not necessarily any corresponding loss of self-esteem when we renowned our weaknesses. Or even positive self-efficacy won't result in higher self-esteem whilst an undertaking is straightforward or unsightly. To quote Bandura's instance, someone is probably very good at evicting people from their homes when they are able to pay their rent or loan, but that skill may not cause advantageous feelings of vanity. This idea became the basis for the conventional tale A Christmas Carol, presenting the character Ebenezer Scrooge.

The development of self-efficacy

Young kids have little knowledge of what they can and can't do, so the improvement of practical self-efficacy is a totally important procedure: Very young children lack knowledge of their very own abilities and the demands and potential risks of different courses of motion. They would repeatedly get themselves into risky predicaments were it now not for the steerage of others. They are able to climb to excessive locations, wander into rivers or deep pools, and wield sharp knives earlier than they develop the important skills for dealing with such situations appropriately. Grownup watchfulness and guidance see younger children thru this early formative duration till they benefit enough understanding of what they can do and what one-of-a-kind conditions require in the manner of competencies.

For the duration of infancy, the improvement of perceived causal efficacy, in other phrases the perception that one has affected the world with the aid of one's own moves, appears to be an vital aspect of developing a sense of self. as the little one interacts with its surroundings, the toddler is capable of motive predictable events, consisting of the sound that accompanies shaking a rattle. The expertise that one's very own movements can have an impact on the environment is something Bandura refers to as non-public enterprise, the capability to act as an agent of change in a single's own global. The infant additionally starts off evolved to enjoy that positive events affect fashions differently than the child. As an instance, if a model touches a warm range it does now not harm the little one, so the little one starts to recognize their uniqueness, their real life as an individual. Throughout this period, interactions with the bodily environment may be more vital than social interactions, since the physical environment is extra predictable, and consequently less difficult to find out about. Quickly, but, social interplay becomes particularly influential.

No longer handiest does the kid analyze a high-quality deal from the circle of relatives, but as they develop peers become increasingly critical. As the child's global expands, peers convey with them a broadening of self-efficacy studies. This could have both high quality and poor consequences. Peers who are maximum skilled and competent can emerge as essential models of conduct. However, if a baby perceives themselves as socially inefficacious, but does broaden self-efficacy in coercive, competitive conduct, then that baby is probable to end up a bully. In the midst of this attempt to examine socially suited conduct, most children additionally start attending faculty, wherein the primary cognizance is on the development of cognitive efficacy. For many children, unfortunately, the academic environment of school is an assignment. Kids quick discover ways to rank themselves (grades assist, each excellent and bad), and youngsters who do poorly can lose the experience of self-efficacy that is necessary for persisted attempt at college. In keeping with Bandura, it is important that instructional practices focus not simplest at the content they provide, however additionally on what they do to children's beliefs about their capabilities.

As kids keep through early life in the direction of adulthood, they need to assume duty for themselves in all elements of lifestyles. They need to grasp many new skills, and a feel of confidence in operating towards the destiny is dependent on a developing feel of self-efficacy supported with the aid of past studies of mastery. In adulthood, a healthful and practical feel of self-efficacy gives the motivation vital to pursue achievement in one's life. Poorly equipped adults, wracked with self-doubt, regularly find existence stressful and depressing. Even psychologically healthy adults have to ultimately face the realities of growing old, and the inevitable decline in physical repute. There may be little proof, however, for large declines in intellectual states till very superior antique age. In cultures that admire adolescents, there may well be an inclination for the elderly to lose their sense of self-efficacy and start an inexorable decline closer to loss of life. However in societies that sell self-growth for the duration of life, and who respect elders for his or her expertise and enjoy, there may be capacity for aged individuals to hold living efficient and self-gratifying lives.

Behavior amendment

In concepts of conduct amendment, Bandura shows that behavioral processes to psychological alternate, whether in medical settings or elsewhere, have an awesome advantage over a number of the other theories which have arisen in psychology. While mental theories often get up first, turn out to be popular as procedures to psychotherapy, however then fail to resist right clinical validation, behavioral procedures have a long history of rigorous laboratory testing. As a result, behavioral strategies are regularly validated first, and then prove to be relevant in clinical settings. Indeed, behavioral and cognitive processes to psychotherapy are usually well reputable amongst psychotherapists (although a few might remember their range incredibly constrained).

Bandura made numerous factors concerning the utility of social studying theory to behaviorally-oriented psychotherapy. As an instance, Bandura notes that the labeling of mental problems, indeed the definition of what constitutes atypical behaviour is made within a social context. Even as it's been tested that not unusual classes of intellectual contamination are visible throughout a extensive sort of cultures we nevertheless view people with psychological issues based on sociocultural norms and, inside the case of too many observers, with unreasonable prejudice. Bandura also adversarial the clinical version of categorizing and treating psychopathology, believing that the preference to perceive and make use of medicinal drugs has hindered the development of applying appropriate psychotherapies. The utility of the ideal therapy involves problems of moral subject and intention-setting. Remedy can't be successful, in step with Bandura, if it does no longer have clean desires characterized in phrases of observable behaviors. deciding on goals approach that one must make treasured judgments; in making those decisions it's miles critical that the patron and the therapist percentage comparable values (or at the least that the therapist work with values appropriate for his or her customer), and that the therapist does not try to impose their own values at the purchaser.

Overall, Bandura presents behavioral procedures to psychotherapy as non-judgmental programs of studying concepts to difficult behavior, behaviours that is not to be viewed as mental "illness:" From a social-mastering angle, behaviors that may be unfavourable to the man or woman or that go away widely from well-known social and ethical norms are taken into consideration not as manifestations of an underlying pathology but as approaches, which the individual has discovered, of managing environmental and self-imposed needs.

The social getting to know environment in which education takes vicinity is called schools or instructional institutions. In these gaining knowledge of areas, there are some of curricular issues and problems faced which can range from moderate to intense. These troubles or problems include the first-rate of conversation within the school room and instructors' isolation. They're of tremendous challenge due to the fact they will have an effect on both teachers and college students negatively, and as a result, learning can be affected.

The first-rate of conversation inside the study room may be demotivating or uplifting. Conversations within the school room must be that of which to educate and be an average of advantage to all. They should be directed most effective to the challenge mentioned.

Instructors' isolation can also affect college students negatively. While teachers are remote, and rely handiest on what they were taught and agree with, they're proscribing themselves and the scholars from acquiring knowledge that can be crucial to them. It's far vital for instructors to partner and collaborate with others due to the fact in doing so, they could advantage information of things they in no way knew, and enhance their capacity to work by myself in addition to a team player.

Those issues will affect students' learning procedure negatively. This could affect now not simply their school life but also their expert existence and their communique skills. They may have little knowledge of a way to express themselves in a way this is appropriate. Instructors can also be affected negatively, and may be restricted as nicely. It will restrict the information in which they communicate unto others, and impacts their potential to be effective teachers.

A few motives for the fine of communication inside the lecture room are due to the fact instructors do no longer set standards within the lecture room, due to the fact college students do not apprehend how to talk, because teachers do not supply students a time in which to make comments and additionally, due to the fact each instructors and students have interaction in conversations which are irrelevant.

Some of the reasons for instructors' isolation are that some instructors consider best the expertise that they possess, and they on occasion feel threatened knowing that other humans are extra informed about some things, especially if is associated with their area of observe.

In order to resolve the communique issue, instructors need to set a particular time in which college students can be engaged, students also want to receive an allocated time in which to make contributions and have to be recommended to stick to the topic/s this is being discussed.

To remedy the problem of teachers' isolation, instructors need to wait obligatory workshops and seminars where they may analyze the importance of teamwork and communication competencies, and they should be have interaction in non-stop training and be assessed frequently.

Chapter Eight

Gender and Development

Gender is a complicated variable that is a part of social, cultural, financial and political contexts. It's also applicable for the work of civil society movements. Gender refers to socially built variations among ladies and men, while intercourse refers to biological differences among males and females. Being socially built gender variations range relying on age, marital fame, faith, ethnicity, culture, race, and sophistication/caste and so on. Sexual differences range little throughout these variables.

Improvement analysts have diagnosed now for numerous decades the need to ensure that gender is examined and incorporated into improvement projects. In integrating gender into development, practitioners are responding to the priority wishes of ladies and men, and being aware of what blessings or detrimental outcomes should effect either.

Why is Gender relevant for improvement?
In taking account of gender, development practitioners and social motion activists are searching at disparities that exist in male and girl rights, obligations, get admission to and manage over resources, and voice at family, network and country wide ranges. Males and females often have unique priorities, constraints and possibilities with recognize to development and can make contributions to,

and be affected differently by, development tasks and campaigning interventions. To decorate effectiveness, those concerns should be addressed in all application and marketing campaign layout and interventions. If such issues are not addressed thoughtfully and competently, those interventions can lead not most effective to inefficient and unsustainable results, but may additionally exacerbate present inequities. Information gender problems can allow projects to take account of these and build in ability to deal with inequitable affects and to make sure sustainability.

When we speak about Gender Equality, we are regarding an aggregate of prison equality and identical opportunities including opportunities to talk out. Extra frequently, which is approximately making better possibilities in all of these areas for ladies. Ladies' rights are protected by using many worldwide devices and laws. The excellent regarded might be the conference for removal of Discrimination towards ladies (CEDAW, 1979) – a UN Treaty adopted with the aid of the general meeting in 1979 and signed initially with the aid of 64 states in July the subsequent year. An elective protocol became later advanced starting up a mechanism through which states would be held responsible to the treaty. There had been subsequent international declarations and pledges that have been used as bench marks to measure development when it comes to specific women's issues. These encompass the Beijing declaration and Platform for motion (1995), and the Millennium improvement desires (2001) which consist of gender concerns in nearly half of the clauses. The MDGs have been together reinforcing; progress toward one goal impacts progress closer to the others. But, the third purpose addresses gender equality especially. The successor Sustainable improvement goals (SDGs), due to be followed in 2015, as a part of a wide sustainable development time table, consists of reaching 'gender equality and empower all girls and ladies' as the proposed goal five.

Ancient traits in integrating gender into improvement
An early technique involved focused on girls by project layout and interventions which centered on women as a separate group. This was typically known as WID (women in development). Critics of this approach talked about that this did now not deal with men, and a later model typically known as GAD (Gender and improvement) focused greater on assignment design and interventions that had been focused on a development technique that transforms gender members of the family. This aimed to allow ladies to take part on a same basis with men in figuring out their not unusual destiny. The Gender Equality approach is therefore about males and females and is for this reason a more complete technique to evaluation and design of development interventions because it takes under consideration the state of affairs and desires of each women and men. It pursuits to contain each males and females in addressing their improvement troubles, to reform institutions to establish identical rights and opportunities, and to foster monetary development which strengthens identical participation. Such an approach pursuits to redress persistent disparities in get admission to sources and the capability to speak out.

Masculinities
It has also been diagnosed by means of specialists and

activists in this discipline that the behaviour of men desires to be addressed inside the context of gender work. Unless men project themselves as to the approaches in which their personal behaviour, attitudes and upbringing perpetuates gender inequality, gender injustice and gender violence, nothing will change. For more than two a long time now, a growing number of programmes addressing those issues were advanced in various parts of the world and the gaining knowledge of shared and tailored to new contexts. The various maximum well-known have been the programmes of Puntos de Encuentro and Cantera in Nicaragua, and its programmes on male behaviour alternate. some other instance, Stepping Stones, a small group intervention the usage of participatory learning to assist enhance sexual health, began in Uganda but become tailored for unique nations throughout sub Saharan Africa together with Gambia, Ghana, Kenya, South Africa, Tanzania and Zambia, in addition to for the Philippines. Its network training package deal "ambitions to encourage communities to impeach and rectify the gender inequalities that make a contribution to HIV/AIDS, gender based violence and other issues" and once more targeted on behaviour change.

Gender and social moves

For the duration of the globe humans are organizing both to assignment and quit gender injustice in all areas of our social, financial, political, and cultural lives. To be successful, but, those struggles want to encompass and priorities gender equality within their very own organizational systems in addition to being part of the analysis and method for trade. That is a deeply political trouble at a ramification of ranges. Even though social moves are trying to address this, activists nevertheless come up against strong resistance to converting gendered politics and practices even within the contexts of actions and allied businesses. Nonetheless, in relation to making an effect on remodeling gender electricity relations, social actions are important.

Integrating gender perspectives into social movements and activism is not just about 'together with' ladies or 'thinking about' guys and gender minorities. It means thinking about what a gendered politics affords in phrases of opportunity ways of being, seeing and doing that in themselves serve to transform patriarchal electricity members of the family. girls' rights and gender justice issues had been approached in a variety of approaches by way of exceptional social movements, but a few commonplace parameters can be outlined which facilitate a supportive surroundings for gender-simply motion building. for instance, declaring the importance of tackling gender inequality and patriarchal power as an crucial aspect of justice and naming this as an express precedence; attractive definitely in inner mirrored image and motion on girls' rights and gender justice, imparting guide for women's leadership and participation in all components of social moves, tackling gender primarily based violence and harassment. Making sure equal position/rank distribution in organizational structures, ensuring participation is identical, taking account of worrying for circle of relatives' contributors, taking account of the reality that girls can be centered in retaliation by way of the ones in society who experience threatened by gender justice as a change to traditional roles.

Gender is an important consideration in development. It is a manner of searching at how social norms and power structures effect on the lives and possibilities available to one-of-a-kind corporations of men and women. Globally, extra girls than guys live in poverty. Women also are less probable than men to receive fundamental schooling and to be appointed to a political function nationally and the world over. expertise that ladies and men, boys and ladies revel in poverty differently and face exceptional barriers in gaining access to services, economic assets and political possibilities help to target interventions.

Gender and why does it count number

Earlier than challenge a gender evaluation, it's far vital to apprehend the concept of 'gender'. According to the sector improvement record (WDR) 2012, gender is described as socially built norms and ideologies which determine the behaviour and actions of ladies and men. Know-how these gender family members and the strength dynamics behind them is a prerequisite for know-how people' get right of entry to and distribution of resources, the capability to make decisions and the manner men and women, boys and women are tormented by political processes and social development.

In comparison with men, ladies manipulate fewer political and economic resources, which include land, employment and traditional positions of authority. Acknowledging and incorporating those gender inequalities into programmes and analyses is therefore extremely vital, both from a human rights angle and to maximize effect and socioeconomic improvement. The WDR 2012 highlights the importance of without delay targeting the persistent constraints and barriers to women's equality (in particular in regions of economic empowerment, academic gaps, household/societal voice, and violence towards girls) so that you can decorate productivity and enhance longer-time period improvement outcomes. Gender equality is likewise critical for sustainable peace, and there is a growing frame of empirical evidence suggesting that a better stage of gender inequality is related to higher risks of inner warfare.

Gender Equality and development, global bank

Let us take a look at how extra gender equality can beautify productiveness, improve development results for the subsequent generation, and make establishments more representative. Markets, establishments, and families play a role in decreasing inequality, and globalization can provide essential possibilities. Home actors want to awareness on reducing lady mortality, narrowing schooling and earnings disparities, growing girls' voice, and restricting gender inequality across generations. The international community needs to make sure consistent guide, improve the availability of gender-disaggregated data, and expand partnerships past governments and improvement groups.

The development of gender on the international schedule

The idea of gender emerged with Ester Boserup's influential work inside the early Nineteen Seventies which challenged the notion of ladies as passive beneficiaries of improvement. She known as for a focal point on women in improvement (WID), to renowned the contributions of ladies' regularly invisible labour. Following frustration with the gradual development of WID, other strategies emerged that criticized the WID approach as being one of sincerely 'add women and stir'. The ladies and development (WAD) technique emphasized the need for structural changes in the worldwide political financial system.

The Gender and improvement (GAD) approach followed, focusing on large inequities and unequal family members. GAD advocates known as for a deeper knowledge of the socially built basis of gender differences and the way this impacts on relationships between women and men. They argued for an advanced expertise of electricity relations and the gendered nature of systems and establishments which impact on the lives of males and females. in place of incorporating women into the cutting-edge patriarchal system, GAD advocates argue for the transformation of the gadget into one characterized by using gender equality.

In addition, states have continued to name for progress towards gender equality via some of global agreements, regional platforms and conferences. at the 1995 fourth international conference on women in Beijing, the maximum influential convention so far, states devoted themselves (inside the Beijing Platform for motion) to organizing mechanisms to promote women's rights – inclusive of country wide motion plans, gender strategies and prison frameworks.

In 2000, states confirmed their commitment to decreasing gender inequalities via the united international locations Millennium declaration. This turned into articulated particularly in Millennium development aim (MDG) three which called for the promotion of gender equality and women's empowerment. three indicators were chosen to symbolize this goal: i) the ratios of girls to boys in primary, secondary and tertiary training; ii) the share of girls in salary employment in the non-agricultural quarter; and iii) the proportion of seats held by using women in country wide parliament. Gender equality is likewise vital which will acquire the opposite seven MDGs. in the submit-2015 procedure to determine what goals, if any, ought to comply with the MDGs, gender has remained a center situation. a few advocates have called for a standalone goal on gender, while others have promoted gender objectives inside every purpose.

Even as development has been made to spotlight women's problems and stories in development programmes, country wide legal guidelines and political choices, attention to gender is frequently inconsistent. In addition, insufficient finances are allocated to ensure that gender equality is an critical a part of these programmes and regulations. Many scholars and practitioners argue that the aim of the 'gender agenda' – the transformation of unequal, unjust electricity relations – has been in large part unnoticed.

Whilst excessive nice data is generally difficult to return by way of in developing countries, it's miles even much less commonplace that excessive pleasant intercourse-disaggregated records is available. Specially, information associated with women's contributions in the casual economy, gender-based totally violence and harmful conventional practices could be very uncommon. This makes it difficult to absolutely understand the stories of men and women and to ensure that programmes are focused wherein they can be most effective. In addition, statistics disaggregated by age is also now and again available, making it difficult to recognize differences among girls and ladies, and men and boys. a few studies and opinions of development programmes have depended on qualitative records in place of quantitative facts. This reliance is criticized by way of some corporations as no longer being rigorous sufficient.

It is important to well known, however, that gender- and age-disaggregation of information is only the first step. Statistics and analysis of the strength differentials or underlying reasons for those differences is likewise wished. Preferably, what is required is a mix of quantitative and qualitative information and analysis that affords evidence of what the differences are and why those variations exist.

Gender members of the family and standing inside the household

Gender members of the family are upheld by using each casual and formal institutions. Informal establishments are typically known as "lengthy-lasting codes of conduct, norms, traditions that make a contribution to gender inequality in all spheres of life". Formal establishments (financial, political, criminal and social) include political structures and labour markets. Those spheres engage with local cultures to determine gender consequences. Social establishments that have been recognized as especially poor for ladies and girls encompass discriminatory family codes, son bias, physical lack of confidence, confined useful resource rights and entitlements, and cultural regulations on ladies' movement and other liberties. Formal establishments can have both meant and accidental negative influences on ladies. As an example, legal guidelines, which includes Shariah, which especially nation that a man's and a woman's witness are of various value have an meant discriminatory impact. A coverage which calls for land titles as a precondition for receiving agricultural credit score may additionally have the accidental impact of except women due to the fact land ownership is usually concentrated among male family members. Taking into consideration the position of two names (a husband's and other halves) on land titles may want to help to cope with this problem.

Development change by way of building Social establishments

Do social establishments result in gender differences within the incidence of poverty? We find that discriminatory circle of relatives codes, son bias, restrained aid entitlements, bodily insecurity and restrained civil liberties play a position in continual poverty, particularly that of young girls. It's consequently critical to: do away with gender discrimination through criminal provisions; guide ladies' participation in choice-making; invest in baby- and gender-touchy social safety; extend offerings to tough-to-attain women; enhance women' aid get entry to; and sell ladies' control over their bodies.

Gender family members through the lifecycle

Gender dynamics and members of the family trade throughout the course of the lifecycle. Popularity within the household is regularly determined by using age, marriage, range of kids, disability, economic sources and academic level attained. ladies, which includes adolescent ladies, regularly have the bottom repute inside the household, mainly in societies in which families need to pay dowry and in which the daughters are sent to stay with the husband's family upon marriage. recent research has identified adolescent girls as mainly vulnerable and susceptible to gender-based totally discrimination along with sexual violence, pressured and early marriage, losing out of college and chance of death all through childbirth. Early marriage and early pregnancy can have unfavourable results on girls' fitness, and can inhibit their capacity to take advantage of educational and task possibilities.

Daughters-in-law and unmarried women are also considered to have low repute in a few cultures as they're visible as outsiders or burdens on the circle of relatives. Widows and married girls who have been abandoned through their husbands may also face stigma and lack of repute.

Families frequently pick out to spend money on boys because the destiny earners and caretakers of the family. This allows boys to grow up having higher repute in the family than ladies and higher earnings generating opportunities. Whilst fame normally increases in line with age for each men and women, it will increase disproportionally for men.

Family roles

Family status determines the jobs of various circle of relatives' contributors. men are regularly assumed to be the head of the family and liable for imparting financially for the own family, at the same time as girls and ladies are responsible for household chores, together with caring for kids, cleansing, fetching water and cooking. at the same time as girls are actually increasingly more capable of take up paid employment, this often does not involve a discount of their home responsibilities, main to the 'double burden' of girls' domestic and productive roles. The time required to carry out home chores additionally limits women's get right of entry to to paid employment and their participation in civil society and politics.

Even as investing in boys' schooling is often viewed as an extended-time period method, the stress on guys to earn money can in a few times lead to boys being taken out of college to assist aid the own family financially. Girls, then again, are much more likely to be taken out of faculty because the family is not able to have enough money their faculty charges and/or relies on girls to assist with domestic chores and childcare.

Even though it is frequently assumed that families are headed by means of adult males, this is not always the case. In conditions of conflict, displacement, labour migration or abandonment, female-headed households may be greater common. These are frequently a few of the poorest and maximum prone households.

Marriage, Motherhood and Masculinity inside the international financial system

Is the rise of ladies within the labour market converting the notion in their position in the domestic? This observe explores how males and females are handling the feminization of labour markets inside the face of the superiority of male breadwinner ideologies and the plain chance to male authority represented by way of women's profits. It indicates that maximum operating ladies preserve to undergo a disproportionate burden of home duty. Ladies may be the use of their newly obtained earning power to undertaking the injustice of the double work burden, but policymakers are still failing to provide aid for ladies' care obligations.

While no longer continually the case, guys are greater normally the heads of the household and the breadwinners of the own family. This has frequently translated into guys making the circle of relatives' economic and non-monetary decisions – together with while daughters get married and to whom, whether the wife can work out of doors of the household, whether or not to apply birth control and who receives the most food. In agricultural societies in which ladies frequently do maximum of the work, male circle of relatives' contributors frequently very own the land and make the agricultural selections. Due to girls' decrease bargaining role inside the family, their choice-making is often constrained and may be limited to childrearing issues and domestic obligations. Elements that exacerbate women's low bargaining positions encompass huge age gaps among husband and wife, which accentuate already existing gender inequalities, cultural elements that devalue girls' unpaid work, lower levels of schooling and financial dependence.

Ladies have in some times been able to find approaches of negotiating control over resources and selection making. Ladies are regularly tasked with budgeting for the household either thru resources supplied through the husband or thru petty trading and agricultural labour. In some instances, ladies are visible as family economic managers. In other instances, whilst ladies won't control the household earnings, they adopt numerous techniques to make certain they could get entry to part of these sources. These may additionally encompass hiding money and lying about expenses, to ensure that they could pay for food and children's education. Interventions aimed explicitly at strengthening ladies' manage over assets, inclusive of conditional coins transfers, may be especially useful.

The Gendered Politics of Farm family production and the Shaping of girls' Livelihood

Unequal strength members of the family do now not fall only alongside gender strains. In addition to gender, individuals can be discriminated towards for some of motives which includes ethnicity and race, faith, caste, age, incapacity, sexual orientation, socioeconomic reputation and geographic vicinity. When gender intersects with other axes of marginalization, girls are much more likely to enjoy a couple of layers of discrimination. In some cases, those other sorts of discrimination may be greater excessive than gender discrimination. An ethnic minority guy can be much less powerful and extra discriminated towards than a center magnificence woman from a majority ethnic institution, despite the fact that a lady from this identical ethnic minority group may want to face even extra discrimination.

Intersectionality is a tool used to better recognize how those discriminations materialize and intersect. It's based totally on an knowledge that ladies and men have layered identities which have resulted from social relations, records and energy systems. Through a deeper appreciation of more than one identities and consequent styles of discrimination, extra powerful responses can be tailor-made.

Gender analyses and programmes have frequently come to

define gender as 'girls', forgetting or ignoring the different approaches wherein men and boys are tormented by gender energy systems and structures and the way this intersects with specific axes of energy. Like girls, guys play various roles in society, the economy and household. Guys have multiple 'masculinities', a number of which involve dominance and others subordination. Recent discussions of masculinity have emphasized the want to have interaction with the systems that maintain gender inequality.

Excluding boys and guys from gender evaluation reduces the effect interventions could have on gender inequality. putting the stress on ladies because the simplest agents of exchange can also be taken into consideration an ethical problem, given the range of different challenges that bad ladies are compelled to confront.

Wherein guys and boys are included in analysis, they're often framed as troubles, rather than as fantastic actors. For instance, unemployment and the structural exclusion of younger guys has been linked to a multiplied danger of engagement in violence. Young men in such instances are often perceived as a protection hazard. In lots of contexts, however, young people who suffer from exclusion do no longer get worried in violence and can be superb marketers of exchange.

Similarly, older men are often visible as boundaries to girls' empowerment. While small-scale programmes that work with guys and boys reveal some achievement toward extra gender equitable attitudes, that specialize in or which include boys and guys remains arguable. Some feminists fear that such a focal point diverts each attention and resources away from women's rights work.

It is turning into increasingly more mentioned that there is a need to better recognize how the gendered identities of boys and guys are shaped and how they can be higher mobilized as a pressure for gender equality. As an example, Australia's country wide motion Plan on girls, Peace and security highlights the significance of male champions in ensuring the safety of ladies and girls. Men and boys can be powerful advocates for gender equality, helping to lessen and prevent violence in opposition to girls and make sure that ladies' wishes are taken under consideration and included as essential factors in peace negotiations and at worldwide fora.

Gender analysis and mainstreaming

Countrywide governments and donors have developed a number of strategies, equipment and sources to make sure their development programmes take account of gender inequality. These strategies include organizational gender mainstreaming, accomplishing gender evaluation, and gender assessments to determine effects of programmes, strategies and laws.

Development in imposing those techniques and as a result growing gender attention and gender equality has been sluggish and advert hoc. Motives for this include a lack of commitment on behalf of stakeholders and insufficient useful resource allocation. Gaps within the series, compilation and reporting of gender-touchy statistics additionally present a substantial venture to powerful gender analysis. at the same time as gender problems are often stated as essential, states and donors frequently supply them decrease priority, considering other aspects of development – along with democracy, poverty or conflict

– extra urgent.

Gender analysis and checks

Gender evaluation is the system of assessing the effect that a improvement programme can also have on males and females and on gender relations in well-known. Gender analysis can be used for a number of reasons inclusive of: i) to make sure that ladies and men are not deprived via any unique activities or strategies; ii) to become aware of precedence areas for movement to sell equality; iii) to assess gendered variations in participation or resource allocation; and iv) to construct capability and dedication to gender equality.

A number of tools had been evolved to assess gender equality development within corporations and programmes. these consist of: i) participatory gender audits, which intention to promote organizational getting to know on a way to almost and efficiently mainstream gender; ii) venture toolkits which include checklists that are lists of inquiries to help programme workforce keep in mind gender variations and capacity gendered affects; and iii) scorecards which include concrete performance signs to evaluate progress. Maximum improvement groups have evolved their personal gender analysis equipment to healthy their needs.

Gender mainstreaming

Gender mainstreaming is the manner of making sure that gender is considered always, both within groups (institutionally) and programmes (operationally). As those are closely interlinked, gender mainstreaming must be implemented each institutionally and operationally to achieve success. A donor agency unable to understand the demanding situations confronted by its own lady staff, for example, would conflict to apprehend the gender impacts of its programmes.

Due to the fact committing to the Beijing Platform for motion, most donors, countrywide governments and NGOs have installed place gender mainstreaming guidelines. Some donors have additionally incorporated different intersections of discrimination: UNHCR's Age, Gender, and variety Mainstreaming approach are taken into consideration as an example of global excellent exercise.

However, progress with gender mainstreaming stays inconsistent, and frequently suffers from inadequate commitment (usually from senior control), inadequate useful resource allocation and insufficient knowledge of gender problems via personnel at all tiers. as an example, an evaluation of gender mainstreaming in UNHABITAT determined that whilst the agency has sought to mainstream gender into middle regions of its work, those efforts aren't uniform in strength throughout the organization. similarly, a key task of gender mainstreaming is the possibility that if gender is a situation to all personnel (as opposed to a selected gender unit), there may be a tendency for no one to surely draw interest to gender issues and to take action. To counteract this problem, gender specialists now advise a dual-song technique the use of both mainstreaming and gender-centered units.

- Gender mainstreaming on Eldis
- Girls residing beneath Muslim legal guidelines
- The due to the fact i am a woman series by Plan worldwide

- The phase of the world financial institution's internet site on gender tools.

Gender and development

Gender equality is considered a critical detail in reaching decent Work for All men and women, with the intention to impact social and institutional change that ends in sustainable development with equity and growth. Gender equality refers to same rights, duties and opportunities that all persons need to experience, regardless of whether or not one is born male or female.

Inside the context of the arena of work, equality between ladies and men includes the subsequent elements:
- Equality of opportunity and remedy in employment
- Equal remuneration for work of equal value
- Identical access to safe and healthy operating environments and to social security
- Equality in affiliation and collective bargaining
- Equality in acquiring meaningful profession development
- A balance among work and domestic lifestyles that is fair to both men and women
- Identical participation in choice-making in any respect levels

Given that women are generally in a deprived function in the place of job as compared to men, merchandising of gender equality implies explicit interest to ladies' needs and views. at the equal time, there are also great poor effects of unequal electricity members of the family and expectations on men and boys due to stereotyping about what it way to be a male. Rather, each ladies and men, and boys and girls, ought to be unfastened to expand their abilities and make selections – without limitations set by way of rigid gender roles and prejudices – based totally on private pastimes and capacities.

The ILO has adopted an integrated technique to gender equality and respectable work. This indicates running to decorate identical employment opportunities through measures that still intention to improve girls' get entry to education, abilities education and healthcare – at the same time as taking girls' function in the care economy properly into consideration. Examples of these include implementing measures to assist people stability work and family responsibilities, and imparting administrative center incentives for the availability of childcare and parental depart.

Gender and development are as powerful as they need to be in Kazakhstan. in keeping with a professor of sociology Kriemild Saunders, "the will to understand a program of improvement to cope with poverty inside the third global changed into announced by President Truman in 1949. He pledged that the antique imperialism of exploitation for foreign profit turned into to be replaced with a democratic improvement programme of 'truthful dealing'." the sector has changed rapidly because the preliminary programmes of development have begun and the addition of a gendered factor of view into the discussion makes the subject immeasurably complex and that much more essential. However even a precise definition of gender is elusive. One interpretation of the phrase, in order to be used all through this essay, states that "gender must be acted out, that it's miles rendered perceptible best through repeated styles of behaviour, that Butler phrases overall performance." As a social construct "gender performance is constantly mediated through the cultural norms of particular social organizations." given that the question pertains to the global south, Kazakhstan, who can effortlessly pass because the closing different, as a publish-soviet USA. With its own history, easily fits into the category as evidenced via the container-workplace achievement of the movie Borat.

It's about know-how interests. Without communication, there may be no progress. If the aim of the improvement paradigm is true equality, which is contestable, assumptions about three key agents that at once or in a roundabout way affect the lives of the maximum marginalized segments of a society need to be modified first. This will cause attention to what gender and development mean, and how the nation, civil society actors, the person can interact with the concept of equality. In Kazakhstan, as most anywhere inside the world, gender is a supply of power as well as oppression, and for the maximum marginalized, none of the three actors are doing sufficient. Educational and a leading vital feminist Dr. Wendy courtroom claim that "behavioral styles that upon repetition form norms aren't a count of arbitrary preference, however, are directly associated with a society's hegemonic ideology." however cartoonist Charles Adams shows that "every day is just a phantasm. What's every day for the spider is chaos to the fly." Any debate approximately normality ought to be held with that in mind.

Gender

"Gendered identities, inclusive of the ones inscribed at the frame and sexualities, and are variously built thru languages and a variety of cultural, social, and financial establishments. In looking to apprehend and challenge gender strength members of the family feminism has had to flow beyond any smooth information of an essential sexual being and identification, whether woman or man".

The maximum marginalized in Kazakhstan are both women and men who deny their distress. Like maximum of the arena, divorce charges going up and girls are gaining bargaining power with the burden of their wallets. "As biological future, masculinity is used to refer to the innate characteristics and homes of guys that distinguish men from ladies. in this view, masculinity is guys' nature, and as such helps to explain not most effective variations but also inequalities among ladies and men. guys' political, financial and cultural privileges arise from their 'masculine benefit', as variously meditated in genetic predisposition to aggression (in comparison to the passivity of femininity), bodily power (in evaluation to the weak spot of femininity) and sexual drives (in contrast to the sexual reserve of femininity)." without understanding that gender is built, human beings will not recognize what the development paradigm is supposed to bring about. And insightful quote from the author of "Gosh Boy George, You have to Be tremendously secure in your Masculinity!" phrases the concept of liberal gender as such: "As a girl, I'm a purchaser of masculinities, however i am not more so than guys are; and, like guys, I as a girl am additionally a manufacturer of masculinities and a performer of them. At the same time as the Western schedule of "Gender equality isn't most effective an end in itself, but also a important means to gain sustainable human improvement and the reduction of poverty." The discount of poverty isn't the point; equality is set having the identical opportunities and rights. Cash should not be the key indicator despite the fact that that is exactly what most liberals appear to suppose. Ideas including wellbeing, are gaining authority within instructional circles. Possibly it's due to the vagueness and meaninglessness of the time period. The hassle with liberal development agendas is a monosex know-how, as highlighted by way of Feminists who view "gender relations no longer in terms of opposed poles but as a continuum. In feminism there's adequate scope for one of a kind expressions of gender identity." in terms of the development paradigm, but, "Key monuments in the founding of ladies and development had been the professional UN conferences that historically have performed an important position in mobilizing girls internationally." however the thoughts of those "advocacy and policy conversations commonly refer, now not to leading philosophers and writers which include Judith Butler, Michel Foucault, Donna Haraway, Gayatri Spivak and Liz Grosz, however to United nations documents breezily acknowledged by means of the names of the places in which the final negotiated files had been signed: Rio, Vienna, Cairo, Beijing, et cetera.'" Kazakhstan as a member of the UN and signatory of CEDAW automatically upholds the agreements of Mexico City, 1975, Copenhagen 1980, Nairobi 1985, Beijing 1995. However does that imply something? In step with creator of, Feminist concepts in African Philosophy of tradition "the Western mono-intercourse gadget is designed around white guys' pursuits, wishes and expectations, and it institutionalized these as part of the kingdom machinery. A cursory observe gift-day upper echelons of political management, the judiciary, the company world, and the military confirms this picture within the America, Canada, and Western Europe. Economic, political, judicial, and regulation-enforcement powers are focused within the arms of rich top- and middle-class white men whose monetary status as 'heads of family' relationally quadrupled in significance."

Western liberal feminists need "to give an explanation for men and their behaviour in phrases of their masculinity, however a masculinity which is described as an embodiment of the cultural norms and social pressures that assist to determine the roles, rights, responsibilities and members of the family which might be to be had to and imposed upon men, in evaluation to ladies." Traditions, cultural norms are determined via the people of that way of life. If there are not any courageous souls, to arise to oppression, acts of interference from outside could be seen as a form of aggression. The Soviets' have claimed to have liberated the steppe and central Asian peoples of their backward approaches, but who's to mention what is just and right? Electricity is the query. As my professor says, gender "is a super that remains tenuous because it's miles by no means absolutely internalized, never quite lived as much as" right here it is useful to apprehend Foucauldian biopolitics where "our bodies no longer as static givens, locked into sure organic rhythms, however as fluid web sites of energy and political contestation." Kazakhstan has all the formal places for political debates and discussion, such as a multi-party parliament and at once elected president, but "Foucault sees electricity as immanent in everyday relationships, consisting of economic exchanges, knowledge relationships and sexual relationships. Micro-level practices of strength are taken up in worldwide or macro-degree strategies of domination. Those power performs are made now not thru centralized power, however via a complicated collection of infinitesimal mechanisms." For conservative liberals "the rising rubric of 'men and masculinities' proved remarkably fertile in producing new conversations and connections in terms of a numerous set of troubles and social issues." This makes any discussion at the issue mechanically politically robust. In Kazakhstan, as prescribed by means of the liberal agenda, "energy has end up represented as something that can be bestowed or received rather than a structural relation that is in itself gendered."

It's far essential to apprehend here that this isn't always approximately "simply the distinctive trends of each social institution's specific gender norms, but also the power of the pressure towards conformity, the range of versions in performance suited for each gender and the diploma to which performances reflect internalized beliefs." without reference to records a body politics understanding of the question might be aware "what is uncomfortable in gendered relations. The frame will become an 'impertinent way of understanding'."

The UN expertise of development that objectives the lives of the most marginalized is also the World Bank information, and "women in development (WID) remains hegemonic at the extent of feminist developmental practices." The problem with this technique is it ignores "complicated hyperlinks between health, reproductive life cycles, the worrying economic system, the marketplace economic system, the surroundings and what became increasingly more summarized as globalization were repackaged via technical information into comprehensible development worries. They were put via the UN device of debate and coverage making and came out because the issues that governments may want to conform to, however, lacked the resources and ability to carry out in fact." authorities potential is questioned by this technique, but that it's miles the responsible agent is taken as a given. "If improvement is not engendered, it's far endangered" recommended the 1997 Human improvement document." As Dr. Harcourt factors out, proper know-how of "the evaluation between the lived physical experiences of the violated women and the comfy lives of ladies main gender and development debates evoke an eerie experience of dislocation." Why? Due to the fact a surface-level engagement with development is what led to "the international norm of non-discrimination and equality culminating within the adoption of the United countries convention at the removal of all kinds of discrimination towards girls (CEDAW)". However, the liberal basis of the UN and the arena bank do now not have a actual information of the frame. "Main philosophers, including John Locke in the seventeenth century and Jean

Jacques Rousseau inside the eighteenth century, described guys as individuals innately possessed of certain 'herbal rights'. Ladies, on the other hand, were defined not as individuals, but as participants of men's families and for this reason, at the side of their offspring, under male control." In Kazakhstan, as in most of the worldwide South wherein the development agenda is absolutely taking its route, "there are uncomfortable contradictions on the center of the body politics of improvement in which the ones described as economically negative are dealt with as gadgets in place of subjects of their personal lives. On paper improvement is delivered in interventions that are smooth, cutting-edge, politically loose, based totally on contemporary technical expertise, sound public health systems and complete economic planning. The truth is some distance, some distance messier." present-day Kazakhstan is falling into the liberal entice of gender expertise, wherein "guys generally tend not to think of themselves as 'gendered' beings, and this is one reason why policy makers and development practitioners, both males and females, regularly misunderstand or push aside 'gender' as a girls' problem." But that is juxtaposed by means of another view, which "in figuring out the non-universality of modernity, points to the reality that, in spite of repeated disasters, the parable of improvement continues to be perpetuated and failures are given circumstantial factors."

Equality

It makes no feel to speak of effectiveness, if there is no idea of what impact is supposed to be. As Saunders points out what is clear is that from the very founding of girls, gender and improvement the 'women's point of view' become no longer singular however heterogeneous and more than one. This maintains to represent a undertaking to the dominant Western feminist will to put in force a gynocentric philosophy and exercise, which centers and magnifies patriarchal power and marginalizes different vertical social members of the family." every other point of view could be that "structurally, this political structure of sex differentiation is one in which girls' and men's pursuits had been institutionalized by way of the nation in order that the heads of the two administrative systems complemented instead of duplicated each differing's powers and privileges." A critical liberal factor of view holds that "culturally brought on physical restrictions caused by high heels, breast implants or the veil - are as a lot part of a gender political struggle in improvement because the demand for equal pay for equal work, gender quotas in parliament or drinkable secure water." It misses out that while real societies are constituted by using intelligent, contradictory, self- and different-influenced complicated personalities, the liberal democratic principles sell a false picture of society as a self-regulating marketplace, populated by means of self-directed, self-stimulated beings whose rational purpose is 'the pursuit of most fabric possessions'" humans are not rational, it's miles a delusion that any of us are. As college of Warwick professor put, in the context of non-Western girls such as Muslim ladies, entire equality as the term has become understood in current-day utilization is hard to deduce from any of the human rights schemes to be had to them." essentially whilst answering the query of effectiveness of the development paradigm, it's miles crucial to be aware that "liberalism cannot claim moral superiority, for the reason that it lacks the grounds to do so." If we're speaking about the said dreams of the improvement paradigm that's equality, what is needed is "a concept of equality that rests on obligation and obligation." As feminist philosopher Nkiru says, ladies did not cost care truly because they were women. They did so because they were moms, sisters, daughters, wives, pals, correct trading companions and so forth. The social ideology of the dual-sex machine did no longer require girls' complete existence to revolve around the care of children and others."

A Kazakhstani understanding of equality is hard to recognize, given the linguistic complexities of the US of a. Nzegwu additionally rightly points out that modern-day Western feminists' critiques of the liberal sociopolitical system emphasize the fact that the language of equality inadequately addresses women's stories in substantive ways." but, whilst equality is framed into a singular chart, so one can be comparable "universalists appear to disregard that their proffered idea of rights and universality has cultural roots, despite the fact that they deal with them as culturally neutral and absolute." Kazakh or some other culture has norms, which are "established 'via a stylized repetition of acts', sediment into an impact of timelessness, commonly referred to as culture. Reiteration gives such sedimentation the arrival of something regular and natural and as soon as this level has been reached it's far handiest a small step earlier than what appears natural acquires regulatory pressure." Who enforces that regulation? The identical individuals who get to jot down them. This leads to the conclusion that the improvement paradigm is useless for the most marginalized in a rustic in which folks that need to put in writing the regulation do no longer recognize how to cross approximately it. Possibly it's far due to the tradition of silence. As in similar cultures, "the capability to talk isn't constant however varies with situations. Nearly each person reviews both situations wherein they are socially authorized to speak and others in which they may be silenced." This suggests that Manifestations in the bodily international aren't all that subjects but "rather that ideology and the fabric scenario are not isolated phenomena however outcomes of the same cultural techniques." In truth, "both ladies and men may be assertive, cowardly, fearless, ambitious, affected person, and smart. Both women and men needed political acumen, foresight, and assertiveness to live to tell the tale inside the sociopolitical conditions of the times and to perform their duties. Oratorical abilities and intellectual acumen described management and have been possessed by using leaders in both institution." it is best "the atypical American cutting-edge political subculture that equates military experience and/or army know-how with political leadership, emphasis introduced Kazakhstan and its human beings have their own tradition. starting with Herodotus, testimonies of Amazon warrior ladies who ruled huge regions of the principal Asian steppes, Tomiris who mercilessly tired the head of her enemy in his very own blood, these are actual pics for human beings in Kazakhstan however are being downplayed through individuals who wish for femininity to be all about tenderness.

The energy and impact of the state cannot be overstated. Especially in an age have been "U.S. militarized regulations inside the post-cold struggle generation have served to reinforce the privileged positions of fellows in choice-making, each inside the US and in different countries." without being aware of the formal choice makers, felony discussions of effectiveness are meaningless. As Kazakhstan develops its policy, it desires to do not forget that following the United States policy is counterproductive. "While any policy approach is militarized, one of the first matters that takes place is that women's voices are silenced. we discover that once America touts any army group as the nice hope for balance, safety, and improvement, the end result is deeply gendered: the politics of masculinity are made to seem "herbal," the male grasp on political influence is tightened, and maximum ladies' access to real political effect shrinks dramatically." Maximum academics appear to agree that despite the fact that many problems persist, the main ones referring to country sovereignty and susceptible and ineffective enforcement mechanisms, a beginning has been made".

Civil society

If the problem of effectiveness may be take a look at through the lens of civil society, perhaps it could be better understood. the majority do not, of route, mechanically comply with behavioural prescriptions but as an alternative are constrained inside a number of norms that are moderate variations on an underlying best that has been inculcated into them from delivery until it bureaucracy an vital a part of their psyche." Consistent with liberal thinkers "thinking of the success of development and the failure of the country to supply, as well as the cease of the cold battle, opened up entry factors for civil society agencies to end up politically engaged in UN worldwide processes. these movements, clustered under the umbrella identify of NGOs, emerged within the 1990s as a third actor within the development community." it is inside the Nineties when impartial Kazakhstan commenced formulating its gender policy, and as responsible country has dutifully signed to ladies' rights files. "Beginning from the UN charter, a wide array of human rights devices promulgated by the UN and nearby organizations included provisions for the protection of women's rights and non-discrimination on the idea of intercourse." Kazakhstan's charter states that everyone international agreements are routinely law on its territory, furnished it does now not contradict the constitution. As such CEDAW can be and has been used as a tool for empowerment for ladies as a social institution. "The implications for states are potentially a ways-attaining. Not handiest have to they abolish all existing discriminatory legislation and practices, they may be additionally obliged to put off stereotyped ideas of male and lady roles in society. Hiding in the back of 'conventional customs and' practices' will now not do. The conference's language is largely Universalist and non-discriminatory, and emphasizes a rights-based framework, representing a huge difference from preceding law that was typically welfares and 'shielding' in tone." right here once more, a familial and contextual information of the development paradigm must provide us pause. "The concept of a twin-sex system society gives upward thrust to a concept of rights that does not involve the extraction of entitlements and the statement of rights against the kingdom. Individuals aren't pitted against the kingdom, and the nation is not seen as an opposed entity".

Man or woman

With regards to real bodies, "we cannot anticipate that marginalized and disempowered people dwelling in the context of a coercive ideology can recognize what is in their own real hobby. They will not be able to reject intricate family members or pick out new ones, even if the idea is that everybody has the proper to pick freely and may gain from these advantages." Kazakhstani women can see themselves as people but "voluntary rational preference and relational autonomy inside an oppressive context might now not get women anywhere." As an understanding of familial values illustrates, although formally, all citizens in the kingdom are people and constitutionally, all residents have same rights are essentially the identical, in truth, now not all human beings inside the society are treated as individuals." perhaps here it makes sense to delve deeper into "systems of gendered oppression, redressing the tendency in current years to awareness mostly on the demanding situations of private trade within person lives." it'd appear that naming the politics of personal/interpersonal family members is a manner both to democratize the personal sphere and to convey every day existence into the political sphere." Democracy isn't always an trouble for the most marginalized. it is the 'increasingly unregulated strength of transnational companies places strategic power inside the fingers of precise corporations of men,' whilst the language of globalization stays gender impartial in order that 'the 'person' of neo-liberal idea has in popular the attributes and hobbies of a male entrepreneur'" even as Kazakhstan can boast of a growing variety of marketers, it's far "experience of disempowerment that probably connects a few ladies and men throughout the patriarchal divide, and gives the possibility of linking a gender politics that challenges patriarchy with a much broader politics of social transformation". If development is more than playing "capture up" it makes feel to focus on real humans. "The body in this experience is a vital political terrain or 'region' for feminist politics. Bodies are not break away politics; certainly, their embodiment – their corporeal, fleshly, material life - determines political members of the family. In calling interest to bodies as political topics, feminists understand that 'we are our bodies'. The political self is not awesome from the body. Our revel in of ourselves, our cultural, political and social identity, is an embodied one, decided by our family members to other our bodies." It is not a rely of if anymore so much as "while ladies understand their 'strength inside' and act collectively with different girls to exercising 'electricity with', that they advantage 'electricity to' act as retailers. Feminist enjoy has shown that this is a manner that may take a variety of pathways, but for which there are not often the kind of brief-cuts envisaged by means of the proponents of empowerment-lite".

Powerful of not, Kazakhstan's most marginalized are surely no longer tormented by the discussion. "this is a debate about gender and power, approximately body politics and political bodies, approximately norms, and hierarchies, about intimate and institutional violence, and about liberation and justice." earlier than the populace as a whole danger an identity crisis, it makes sense to formulate a familial, non-intrusive coverage on gender so that it is able to pursue development. "For instance, writing of occasions in Serbia inside the 1990s, notes that the political and monetary adjustments endangered the male identity a lot extra than the female'. Consequently: New prophets regarded on the scene imparting various socio-organic arguments in support of the claim that men are inherently superior. One such turned into Tosevski, who publicizes Serbian masculinity to be superior to the western variety and advocates open promiscuity for males. Such absurd perspectives can best be taken critically by means of people who lack ideological grounding. The Serbian example additionally "warns us that masculinity is not the belongings of fellows, and reminds us to be wary of the usage of the terms 'men', 'male' and 'masculinity' interchangeably. Discourses of masculinity are to be had to, utilized by and imposed upon each woman and man." Given the shared space, sizeable as Kazakhstan's steppes can be, possibly it makes sense to transport towards a greater "ecological self and a regenerative technique in place of a productive (utilitarian) courting to nature." Kazakhstan is a home for a people, and no person can silence subjective truths approximately equality. What can be remarkable to universalist idealists, is that speaking about violence within the home, rape, repression, and homophobia, or challenging 'traditions' - those who veil ladies, placed their toes in high-heeled footwear, condone and institutionalize inequalities within the place of job or within the public meeting spaces that silence ladies, and build on male fears - those are impertinences to the givens, to the norms and the unstated social and cultural regulations." If family values are extra essential than materialism, then who if not the human beings can task "us to take severely in our theorization the links between Social Corporation and the character of equality"?

Chapter Nine

Culture and the Society

Tradition is the essential a part of the human's society. Everybody is spending his or her lifestyles inside a certain cultural network. It regularly defines what types of character a man or woman is and what values will they've. Does the cultural environment have an instantaneous effect at the values within a community for anthropology, psychology and sociology?

To apprehend it higher, we will in the beginning define what the cultural surroundings are and what has an impact it has on humans within it. The very nature of the cultural environment is cultural and social components. It's far may also be known as "a social context" and occasionally "milieu". It's far a subculture of a society or a group wherein a positive individual is living or getting a schooling; it is establishments and those who engage with a certain human. Through interaction we are able to suggest not simplest exclusive forms of non-public conversation (like on a place of business, in class, with friends and so on.); people can also communicate with each different through manner of various communicational media (like smartphone, net, newspapers, TV and so forth). In spite of non – personal sort of the conversation, people whom a person or a lady meets in net may have an influence on his or her values and factor of view. Additionally television and different mass media shape our perception of existence and different humans step by step. This kind of interaction we can name one – manner or anonymous. It does now not always imply the equality of the social fame. Therefore, the concept of social surroundings is wider than the idea of a social circle or a social magnificence. Nonetheless, it's miles common that the ones humans who've the identical social environment begin having an experience of harmony. They without problems assist and accept as true with each different; also they tend to create a social organization. As a result, the ones people will continually have a similar manner of wondering and comparable patterns although they make special conclusions.

It indicates us that people rely on society and the way of life around them very lots whether or not they apprehend this truth or now not. Allow us to in brief define what culture itself is. It's far going to help us recognize what kind of impact it has at the values within a community for anthropology, psychology and sociology.

There may be plenty of facts about the culture and the different consequences of it. It's impossible to transmit culture through the family tree. Tradition is not something innate; culture is something that everybody has to analyze. One of a kind sides of it are interrelated; a subculture is spread through those people within a group. In recent times unique cultures ought to easily exist within a country facet through aspect (find it irresistible generally happens in African countries). The definition of a way of life is following: "The included sum overall of learned behavioral developments which are occur and shared by means of individuals of society". Culture consists of "age grading, spiritual rituals, and athletic game". There are "traditional variations in assignment and doing enterprise were breaking down and this supposed that standardization in place of edition is turning into more and more normal". Probably, a tradition is one of the maximum vast environmental variables that should be taken into consideration within a international advertising and marketing. Regularly a subculture couldn't be freely left out; it frequently hiding from a view. Tradition includes some elements; they are language, aesthetics, religion, values and attitudes, schooling, social enterprise and material tradition. It's important to speak about in brief each element of it.

Material way of life includes communications, energy, transportations and others. Language is the next factor of the way of life. It is a reflection of the values and nature of a sure society group. It can be sub-cultural languages, for example, dialects; in some international locations, it could be or maybe greater languages. Aesthetics consists of artwork, dancing, arts-tune. It issues true taste, splendor, form, and color of it. Training, as it is simple to see, consists of the transmission of thoughts, attitudes, skills and training in sure disciplines as properly. Furthermore, education serves as a transmitter of cultural and social values. Now and again a toddler became added to the cultural price via faculty or later by university. faith offers the people' behavior the great insight and as well it allows us to answer special questions, as an example, why human beings behave in this manner and not in any other.

We are able to see that "way of life" is a complicate theory; it consists of exclusive components. What can we say approximately "values" thought? What's commonly meant through "values"? Rapidly, via values a person can also suggest something this is clearly matter to him or her. Its beliefs and ideas anyone holds as special. Social and cultural surroundings paperwork one's values. Domestic, church college – there are only a few locations where human beings should examine values that might be commonplace for every person inside their cultural environment. Instructors, friends, dad, and mom are forming our private system of values. As a result, we've personal values. Arts et al. (2003) summarized that they encompass something that we generic from people around us and that part that came with our own existence experience. it's far too compulsory to just accept the whole thing a person is hearing around him or her; though, values of cultural surroundings round us has its robust have an effect on our very own machine of values.

Now, when we apprehend what "values", "lifestyle" and cultural surroundings" normally imply we can look at the direct impact that the cultural surroundings have on the values within a community for anthropology, psychology, and sociology.

Earlier than discussing the have an impact on of a cultural environment on a person according to anthropology let us in short point out the definition of the technology. Saying quickly anthropology is the inquiry of humanity. Its origins throw again within the social sciences, herbal science, and humanities. The term itself is taken from the ancient Greek language and has two components: "man" and "have a look at" or "discourse". The topics of anthropology are "how do humans behave", 'what are their physical tendencies", "why we can see variations and versions between organizations of human beings", and sooner or later "who became the ancestor of the modern-day human beings". Anthropology is generally divided in to four fields; they're cultural, or social, anthropology, linguistic anthropology, archaeology, and organic, or bodily, anthropology. We will see that anthropology itself is the technological know-how that studies social and cultural values, differences, origins, roots, and so forth. For this reason, it is essential to talk approximately the influence of the way of life environment in line with this certain technological know-how.

Consistent with anthropology, a culture can be seated deeply; unprepared person may want to take a few type of a tradition like something senseless, peculiar or even cruel. let us supply an instance. Consistent with the Muslim subculture a female ought to cowl her face with yashmak and disguise herself from any alien. Nilaweera & Wijetunga (2005) emphasized that this custom should appear ordinary and senseless to any character from Europe, the USA, or numeral other countries in which people flaunt a woman's form brazenly. Here is another instance of the alternative tradition. In some African nations (like Congo, Kenya, etc) women do now not wear top clothes. Oyeshile (2004) explained this truth that in keeping with their tradition, their traditions, and in keeping with their hot climate they do now not remember the pinnacle of the woman body something that they have to cowl or conceal. There are numerous different one-of-a-kind examples of factors and customs which are unacceptable and even crook in one part of the arena; at the equal time at every other part of it, human beings don't forget the tradition and generally do it.

Summarizing this brief extract we are able to see those cultural surroundings have a direct impact on the values inside a community for anthropology. Maintain the two examples above, a girl from the African United States where there is not commonplace or obligatory to cowl her frame with upper put on have values that are exclusive from the values which are precious for a girl from a Muslim United States of America. If the ones girls should try and explain themselves their way of life, values and motives why they're preserving those culture values they could rarely understand every different. It is common that Muslim people condemn girls from Europe and the US. For them, even the most modest and limited American woman appears to be a girl without way of life values due to the fact she suggests certain part of her body

What can we say approximately the impact of the social surroundings on personal values for psychology? What's psychology? It is the science of human behavior and the mind. This science is a try and understands humanity by using exploring sure particular instances and through coming across some well-known concepts as nicely. One of the main desires of psychology is to advantage society. Scientists who worried in it we can divide in to a few companies: cognitive scientists, social scientists, and behavioral scientists. Amongst others, social conduct is among different topics of psychology. The technological know-how of psychology explores the following principles: emotion, cognition, phenomenology, belief, and interest, mental functioning, conduct, motivation, persona, unconscious thoughts, and interpersonal relationships. As anthropology, the science of psychology is a social technology and it has a robust connection with social surroundings. Consistent with psychology, some type of conduct may be taken into consideration ordinary and other types might be considered ordinary. Usually, humanity has the same nature. For example, murdering and cruelty is taken into consideration peculiar in each social group and community. Though, within some cultures, the thought of cruelty can also range. Allow us to deliver an instance. In American and ECU countries violation in any shape is unacceptable even inside an own family. For this reason folks who maintain doing it to others might consider it psychologically atypical. In line with the tradition of a few Japanese international locations, especially countries with Muslim tradition, a husband can beat his spouse or punish her or in every other way if she does now not fulfill him. What sort of misdeed should a wife do? She may also cook meals that her husband does not like; she can also say a word that her husband ought to keep in mind unacceptable. People in the network with such way of life are taken into consideration psychologically regular despite the fact that they commit violence each day. in line with their culture cruelty is suitable. A lady is expecting it and she or he has no even proper to complain. in keeping with the instance above we are able to see that mental scenarios within a network ought to have a strong terrible impact on the non-public values of a human. a person can observe low values of participants of the network round him or her and subconsciously this man or woman ought to understate the ones values that she or he had before. Psychologically people willing to depend on society. This is why we are able to a country that the cultural surroundings have an instantaneous impact on the values within a community for psychology.

Sociology is the ultimate technological know-how that we

are going to talk about. It studies the society the use of distinctive strategies of essential analysis and empirical investigations. This technology refines and develops information approximately the activity of human society. One of the targets of sociology is to reap the social welfare with the suggestion of the expertise. The sphere of hobbies in sociology varies from the micro-level of interplay and corporation to the macro level of social structures and systems. It is a totally extensive theory this is centered historically on social magnificence, religion, social stratification, social mobility, secularization, deviance and regulation. It includes all spheres of people's pastime. It is interesting that sociology studies specific types of interactions between humans. We are living inside the age of the sector extensive globalization while the entire planet is becoming one huge residence. Exclusive cultural and social communities are not staying become independent from each different adore it became some loads years ago. Human beings are transferring, migrating and spreading their tradition and one-of-a-kind values among other societies.

Why are we able to country that according to sociology, the cultural surroundings have an instantaneous effect on the values within a community? First reason is that humans want to communicate with each other. It approach that they getting some new know-how and values. When representatives of different cultures are staying in touch for some time they may get used to new values. It'll prevent being new for them. New cultural values turns into common and in step with sociology people will begin accepting it in their lives. In a while they could not take into account that one or another subculture or value was not imparted to them. And it's miles the second one cause why the cultural environment has an impact on values of humans for sociology. In other words, whilst people pass from one place to some other they devise a brand new social organization with combined tradition and values.

All factors and elements that we mentioned above we are able to see that anthropology, sociology and psychology are connected among each different. Those three sciences are all about the human nature, culture, and community. they're analyzing interactions and cooperation among different humans; we will kingdom that the cultural environment have an instantaneous impact at the values within a network for anthropology, psychology and sociology due to the fact according to those sciences it's as much as people's nature to take something new from others. in keeping with faith, human society become created as one huge family. allow us to agree that this announcement is right; therefore, we want to accept that people inside a social community have an immediate impact on every other within the identical way wherein participants inside an everyday own family have.

Tradition is the common denominator that makes the moves of the people understandable to a specific institution. This is, the machine of shared values, ideals, behaviors, and artifacts making up a society's manner of existence. Tradition can either be represented in a fabric or non-cloth form. The definitions and particular traits of every of them are mentioned under.

Fabric way of life is a time period related to the physical creations made, used, or shared by way of the contributors of a certain society. It's miles society's buffer in opposition to the surroundings. The components of cloth culture are all the creations (objects) of the humankind and mind, for instance, motors, taps, computer systems, timber, and minerals, just to say but some.

The transformation of raw material into usable forms through the employment of understanding is paramount in the success of material lifestyle. as an instance, we make living abodes to shelter ourselves from the adversities of weather and for our very own privacy on the primary level. Past this, we make, use, and percentage sophisticated, thrilling, and important objects relaying our cultural orientation. For example, the sorts of clothes one wears reflect so much into the way of life we enroll in, like faculty, religion, or where the last excursion changed into spent.

Non-cloth tradition, then again, is the summary or unseen creations achieved via society and normal closer to the behavioral impact of it. The additives of the non-fabric tradition consist of symbols, languages, values, and norms. For example, the activities that society takes element in include things like cricket in India, social establishments, which include churches, faculties, own family, and so on.

The use of language, the styles of behavior, ideals, and values form the route of a society through the years. Language performs a essential part while it comes to steer or perception, values guide and teach us what society has to be like, at the same time as the existing norms form the customs of society.

Language

Language itself is the combination of symbols expressing

thoughts that enable people to think and speak with each other, both verbally or nonverbally. Language allows us to provide an outline of fact, share reports, feelings, and knowledge with different humans.

Using language enables human beings to create visual pix, to differ from outsiders, and as a result, maintain societal harmony and limitations. It also serves as a completely unique tool within the manipulation of symbols for the expression of summary standards and guidelines and, consequently, creating and transmitting way of life between generations.

The aboriginals, as an instance, of their use of language confine to their society, describing relationships instead of judging or comparing. To them, language shapes the truth in notion and enjoy, certainly fronting the thought of neglecting a few components of the arena traditionally viewed as essential. Most of the aboriginal languages do now not abhor the usage of non-public pronouns used to explain gender like she or he, with some amused through the western debate over whether or not God is a He or a She. For this, the impact that the language has on the sector is much less excessive and displays the traditional popularity of a sure place on the sector map.

Via preconceived ideas, the language may also beef up perceptions approximately race and ethnicity in advancing the prevalence of a positive group of people of the rest of the sector. The variety of language in a few parts of the sector shows how it can have an impact on the way of life of the societies in this or that US. Canada is an example of the variations in language these days with Aboriginal, French, and English speaking societies living there.

Language continues cultural historical past and keeps a feel of identity in a subculture. It additionally has the energy of a social manipulate booster with perpetuation of inequalities among people or agencies of humans. The existence of hate in Canadian society is one such state of affairs inflicting plenty of struggling in the US. The aboriginals have a tendency to speak approximately the presence of the English language here and there as a source of energy and prestige. They're additionally mentioning the dearth of films in their language.

Language contributes a exquisite deal to the advancement of both – cloth and non-fabric cultures. Fabric is typically associated with the film enterprise that is, in flip, geared at cost-effective empowering of the lifestyle, at the same time as non-cloth tradition is extra centered on things like heritage and national identification.

Symbols

In each culture, symbols represent the idea of it and signify loads of things that are a fundamental a part of this or that society. Essentially, a cultural image is known as a physical display that demonstrates the ideology of a selected culture, which include religious or ideology beliefs.

A symbol can be an motion, item, or word that stands for a sure summary idea or concept. a few appropriate examples of symbols consist of shades, figures, sounds, and gadgets. For example, people that stay in Hawaii have a tradition to carry out Lua. The latter is the symbol of their place, as well as history that is typically finished through dancing and making a song. What's more, symbols also are represented by way of word interpretations and facial expressions.

It's important to say that the identical symbol will have a completely different that means to exceptional people or organizations of people. For this reason, hypothesizing how this or that way of life goes to symbolize something is not possible. The point here is that some of the symbols is probably gained from subculture, even as others are received from existence enjoy.

Values

Values serve as the other necessary a part of any society on the globe. They encompass judgments of what's applicable or unwanted, what is good and what's awful. The values that exist on this or that society form its norms. As an instance, in Japan, the important thing value is known as group concord.

Mostly, values are received in early adolescence years and are typical of a non-rational nature, even though people would possibly trust that the values that exist in their US are pretty rational. All in all, the values which can be a part of our everyday lifestyles are the cornerstones of our cultural orientation. All of the present cultural values share modern society, in addition to influence all of us that lives inside this or that society. However, the fact is that differences in cultural values among a specific society and people living in you can still end up the primary reasons in the back of the troubles like disagreements, wars, way of life clashes, and so on. What it comes all the way down to is that it is crucial to now not simplest recognize the significance of the prevailing cultural values as a whole but also recognize how critical is the function that all of them play within the life of a positive network.

Norms

Global cultures generally tend to differ substantially of their norms. Frequently, norms are divided into formal and casual ones. As for the formal norms, they're additionally called mores and legal guidelines. The formal norms are related to the standards of conduct that are the most critical in any United States of America. As an example, the US formal norms consist of crook codes, site visitors' laws, and in an academic world, student behavior regulations associated with cheating. As for the norms of the casual kind, they're called customs and folkways. They all are related to behavior requirements that are considered no longer that essential. However, informal norms do have an effect on human beings of a sure society. A common example of casual norms consists of desk manners or the way we communicate with the cashier in our everyday lifestyles.

It is vital to say that lots of norms have a tendency to differ unbelievably from one society or the following. For example, the exceptional evidence of cultural variations can be visible in sexual behavior. While in sure regions in East Africa girls can enjoy sex, the norms that exist inside the other areas call getting satisfaction from intercourse deviant.

When we attempt to understand the cultures that exist these days or the ones from the past, it's far important to recall various factors which can be an indispensable a part of the society that is being tested. Languages are a distinctly important part of any community because it identifies its tradition. Most usually, cultural cognizance refers to symbols as the visual identity, even as discovering values and exploring norms is a defining feature of an active, loose, and wondering character. All in all, beliefs, values, norms, languages, and emblems form the traditions, practices, and establishments of every culture on the globe. They tend to influence all sorts of social structures, social interactions, and social behavior. with a view to get a better expertise of the world around us, it's miles essential to neutrally look at the present beliefs, cultural values, symbols, and norms which can be an necessary a part of social conduct.

There are many cultures out there: educational, professional, countrywide, corporate, non-secular, gender, and so forth. Every one of the cultures noted earlier than have an effect on the lives of humans. Truly, the way we see the world especially consequences from our cultural historical past. We stay in a culture, and we research from it.

There are essential sorts of definitions of the term "tradition": the overall/massive one, called the "anthropological approach", in step with which all human activities are cultural, within the same experience as art, tune, literature, language, customs, faith, meals, homes, furniture, weapons and so on.; the constrained one, wherein handiest intellectual, ethical and aesthetic aspects of human pastime can be known as cultural. The confined definition is extra popular with the common humans however for the scientific societies the entire one is extra suitable. More than hundred definitions of subculture were studied by means of A. Kroeber and C. Kluckholn, who provided us with a useful typology of six kinds of definitions of "culture": enumerative, ancient, mental, genetic, normative, and structural. The primary kind, the enumerative definitions, don't meet the wishes of medical usefulness, are inadequate (too shallow), as it's impossible to list all the spheres and factors of lifestyle and moreover – it isn't always green. For example, a definition by using E. Tylor, an evolutionist, can be supplied. His definition combines factors of enumeration with anthropological conclusions: "lifestyle or civilization is a complex entirety, encompassing knowledge, ideals, artwork, law, morality, customs and all kinds of other competencies and habits received through a member of a society". Ancient definitions represent culture with the usage of key standards consisting of tradition, collective output, historical past, accumulation. The troubles of diffusion of tradition that is its transmission in time and space were examined by using one of the fathers of Polish sociology, Stefan Czarnowski, who claims that "subculture is a whole lot of objectivized factors of the social output of organizations of the identical rank with the aid of virtue of their objectivity, set and able to spreading". "Objectification", the key time period inside the definition, method the existence of cultural entity in its material form, to be had for the receiver. In keeping with this interpretation, the department among fabric subculture and religious one appears useless. Spiritual way of life, consisting of religion, art, song, literature can't exist without their material carriers consisting of temples, liturgical items, artwork, musical rankings, information, and copies of books. at the identical time, cloth culture inclusive of architecture, gear, various patron goods can't come into being without. All quotations translated by Anna Matuchniak-Krasuska. Tradition and Society non-secular background, consisting of planning, designing, developing a recipe for a given product. Cultural censorship, each in the time of Inquisition and throughout Communist regime, was characterized with the aid of persecution and destruction of cultural items together with books (later additionally copies of movies and different information companies) in addition to prohibition to acquire, own, examine or watch. Indexes of forbidden books allowed the existence of or few copies in unique library magazines closed to the public. Anti-communist films had been now not accredited for mass distribution and have been mendacity at the archive shelves for years, gaining a unique call of "shelves". Psychological definitions give attention to socialization and acculturation of the individual that is introducing the individual into lifestyle, its norms, patterns, models, values. Transmission of way of life and mastering it are subjects that border on sociology and psychology. All cloth factors of lifestyle being the products of human beings, and additionally creations of nature that surround us (mountains, rivers, territories, and landscapes) had been called "correlatives" of subculture via Stanisław Ossowski, who reserved defining elements of lifestyle for "attitudes and tendencies in the direction of a particular reaction to correlatives of the way of life". Subculture had in his view only a spiritual this is consciousness related dimension, despite the fact that, obviously, it became observed via the already noted fabric correlatives. Transmission of culture requires on the equal time a switch of the cloth item: a device, a piece of artwork, and suitable attitudes toward the ones items. Loss of data about specs of lace can cause its terrible assessment as simply a material complete of holes. The records of culture are complete of similar examples of an unorthodox evaluation or usage of an item. This trouble applies to intergenerational transmission as well as to intercultural diffusion. Structural definitions, in other words, distributive definitions, are dedicated to the type of culture and the person of every subculture on the whole. "Subculture is fixed of learned behaviors and their outcomes; the elements of which can be common for participants of a given society and are unfold within the society". It is also profitable to cite the shortest definition from R. Benedict: "way of life is a complex entity comprising habits obtained by means of human beings as members of a society". The multitude of formulas of culture determines the wealth of the whole human lifestyle. Those researchers gave arguments to combat ethnocentrism and eurocentrism in order to hold cultural relativism. Genetic definitions, as the name itself, suggests, cope with the rising of the human way of life, the process of anthropogenesis expressed inside the slogan "from nature to a subculture". It isn't always, as in the preceding case, approximately specs of each tradition, however approximately the genesis of it as a time-honored phenomenon.

Tradition additionally refers back to the methods wherein extraordinary organizations of people arrange their everyday lives within country wide or ethnic businesses, city neighborhoods, agencies and professions, and different settings. It includes what humans clearly do and what they consider. It influences greatly how we see the arena, how we attempt to apprehend it and how we communicate with every different. Therefore, tradition determines, to an outstanding extent, learning and coaching styles.

Effect of subculture on worldview

It is stated that someone's way of life and upbringing has a profound impact on how they see the arena and how they procedure facts. Some human beings tended to view the sector in elements or distinct training of gadgets defined with the aid of a set of policies.

In other phrases, in a few international locations, youngsters see the arena in terms of the relationship between things, whereas other youngsters see the world in terms of the objects as wonderful entities. This data is helpful when we take into account how cultural heritage might have an impact on the approach to studying and college overall performance.

Way of life: dad and mom and educators

Parents and educators are privy to the disparities that exist under their personal college residence roofs. Disparities exist in success, investment and readiness. But we cannot be predicted to sufficiently deal with any of these gaps without acknowledging the cultural gaps that live on among students and teachers.

Culture is often perceived as celebrated vacations and recipes, or religious traditions. However at the basis of it, culture is a unique enjoy. Cultural tendencies impact the way youngsters participate in education. To interact college students effectively within the studying process, instructors need to know their students and their academic skills personally, instead of relying on racial or ethnic stereotypes or prior enjoy with different college students of comparable backgrounds.

The definition of ordinary school behaviour may be based totally upon individualist and collectivist cultures. Teachers who lack information about a tradition might misinterpret the conduct of an infant and inaccurately judge students as poorly behaved or disrespectful.

Unique training for these days' teachers: An introduction," say that the impact of way of life at the importance of training and participation styles cannot be overestimated. Many Asian students, for instance, tend to be quiet in class, and making eye touch with teachers is taken into consideration beside the point. In comparison, maximum ECU American youngsters are taught to fee lively classroom dialogue and to look teachers directly in the attention to expose appreciate, even as their instructors view students' participation as a sign of engagement and competence.

Dad and mom from a few Hispanic cultures have a tendency to regard instructors as professionals and could regularly defer academic decision making to them, while ECU American dad and mom are regularly more actively worried in their kids' classrooms, are visible in the lecture rooms, or volunteer and assist instructors those cultural variations in cost and perception may additionally purpose educators to make misguided judgments regarding the fee that non–European American households vicinity on education.

Effect on training

Educators take into account that newbies aren't all of the same. Pat Guild of the Johns Hopkins faculty of schooling says that too often, educators preserve to deal with all learners alike despite the plain cultural range within.

Mora-Bourgeois provides that addressing cultural differences in the teaching-learning manner is each vital and arguable. It's miles vital due to the fact we are faced with an more and more numerous populace of students and the wide success gap among minority and non-minority students. It is debatable due to the fact we may additionally fall into the enticing of cultural stereotyping and making naive attempts to explain achievement variations amongst our college students.

Instructors continue to be the ultimate advocates for studying, but many are not always aware of what their college students address once the dismissal bell has rung. The Southern Poverty regulation middle's teaching Tolerance says that many instructors are white, middle magnificence English speaking individuals. At the same time as instructors commonly are shade blind and that they teach with equity and without discrimination; this practice does no longer constantly address cultural range.

Instructors cannot get away the reality that their conversation "styles" mirror their cultural historical past. plenty of what they say, the way they say it, and their dating with students, dad and mom and co-workers are deeply inspired by using the way they have been socialized. Race and ethnicity frequently play vital roles in children's identities, and contribute to their conduct and their ideals. Spotting this can help students reach a faculty culture in which expectancies and verbal exchange are unfamiliar.

Curriculum

Even the most "widespread" curriculum decides whose

history is worth of study and whose books are worth of analyzing. Guild says that despite the acknowledgment of essential differences among newcomers, uniformity maintains to dominate faculty practices.

Nathaniel Cantor stated in his 1953 eBook "The teaching-studying system," that "the public elementary and high schools, and faculties, normally task what they take into account to be the proper manner of studying that's uniform for all students." In fifty years, many would possibly argue that now not a whole lot has modified. Maximum schools nonetheless feature as though all college students had been the same. Students use the equal textbooks and identical substances for getting to know. They may work at an exclusive tempo, however they take a look at the identical content and work thru the same curriculum. And, of path, schools use the identical tests for all to degree the fulfillment of the studying. Curriculum and text picks must include distinct voices and methods of knowing, experiencing, and understanding existence. In this manner, college students can find and cost their own voices, histories, and cultures.

Variety vs Uniformity

Guild explains that schools are closely biased toward uniformity over variety — typically because sameness is simpler to deal with than difference, and due to the fact educational practices had been advanced to promote fairness for all college students. just a few coaching fashions exist that accommodate each academic values and human range.

Honoring diversity does no longer negate the need for absolutes in schooling. Each learner benefits from a top notch trainer and a fascinating getting to know enjoy. Every scholar and teacher merits to be dealt with appreciate. Each pupil should have a possibility to reach his or her person capability. Each pupil need to grasp specific simple abilities. The challenge is to pick out what have to be the same in colleges and what must be unique.

Uniform standards however no longer standardization

The emphasis on uniformity creates dangers for students whose subculture has taught them behaviors and ideals which might be exceptional from the norms of the majority tradition most customarily emphasized in faculties. College students whose households fee collaboration are advised to be independent. Students whose way of life values spontaneity are informed to workout self- manage. Students who are rewarded of their families for being social are advised to work quietly and on my own. Different cultures include a duality in that kids embody the lifestyle wherein they live however must take on the behaviors essential to come to be upwardly cellular. This cultural conflict often causes battle when individual strengths aren't valued or respected.

How does way of life impact our capability to learn?

When educators think about variety in the study room, way of life may be one of the characteristics that crosses their thoughts, however as they pick their curriculum and broaden their lessons, maximum instructors aren't accounting for a way tradition will impact a scholar's potential to take part and analyze, says Almitra Berry-Jones, Ed.D., nationally recognized speaker, creator, and representative on the subject of culturally and linguistically numerous newcomers at-chance. Cultural Relevance and academic fairness inside the Age of ESSA, Berry-Jones explained how know-how the impact of subculture, adopting a pupil-first mindset, and growing a couple of factors of engagement with the same content will assist instructors pass closer to instructional equity of their study room.

First, Berry-Jones mentioned subculture; the values and beliefs college students convey to the study room. Lifestyle is a social assemble, not genetic, and maximum college students have at least 3: home, peer, and school. The language and behaviors for everyone is exceptional, and for lots college students, the language at home is so divergent that coming into school is like going to a foreign USA and speaking a new language. As an example, college students may come from a domestic in which children are advised to be seen and not heard, so talking up and taking part in magnificence appears wrong to them. Or, what a few teachers see as a conduct disease is just the contrast between the way of life at domestic and at faculty.

Also, educators want to think about students who don't "communicate the language of faculty." there may be a connection between the poverty stage a pupil grows up in, the instructional achievement of the students' mother and father, and language. Poverty frequently creates a developmental burden that manifests in a phrase gap and populations of children who aren't prepared to learn. Extra vital, there may be additionally a remarks gap because most of these children' interactions with adults had been terrible. The scholars arrive in kindergarten now not information the role of the instructor or a way to broaden a nice dating with her or him.

Colleges need to be striving for equity, wherein each learner is getting what she or he desires to be successful. Offering fairness to begin with means know-how the areas of practice that have an impact on the fulfillment hole and the way to tailor lessons to unique studying and cultural wishes.

Concerning literacy, Berry-Jones diagnosed 4 key areas that can effect fulfillment and are stricken by lifestyle:

- Listening and talking
- Questioning
- Analyzing
- Writing

For instance, whilst coming near how college students think, teachers want to keep in mind students' existence experiences before the lecture room, their world view, and the approaches wherein their mind have been shaped by way of their community.

In addition, Berry-Jones advocates for instructors to increase a culturally self-sustaining pedagogy, which requires deliberate practice and practice.

1. First, instructors need education and optimistic remarks to understand how they could improve their abilities; additionally they need to be open to studying new thoughts and strategies.

2. Extra critical, educators should offer consistency and persevere with even the maximum difficult college students. The problem is not that scholars don't want to research, but there are different cultural effects interfering with their capacity to examine. Instructors ought to provide opportunities for college students to percentage their worldview and take the price of their training.

"we will push our freshmen a lot in addition, now not by way of placing an increasing number of records in front of them, but by way of…believing that they are able to do what we're asking them to do and stretching them and giving them opportunities thru discussion," said Berry-Jones. "Allow them to talk peer-to-peer approximately what they're seeing, what they're getting to know, what they're reading. Furthering that conversation is what maintains college students interested and engaged in training. It's no longer our song and dance recurring."

Social Inequalities

Inequality means unfair or not identical in kingdom. Social inequality sounds natural or regular in our US. My objective for this research is to discuss the distinct society's issues about inequalities.

Social inequality is the existence of unequal possibilities and rewards for unique social positions or statuses inside a collection or society. Although America differs from most EU nations which have titled nobility, the U.S. remains relatively stratified. Social inequality has numerous critical dimensions. Income is the profits from work or investments, even as wealth is the whole value of money and different belongings minus money owed. Other crucial dimensions include strength, occupational status, training, ancestry, and race and ethnicity.

There may be no doubt that people inside the U.S. are higher off than most other humans in the international. That being stated, poverty additionally affects millions of people inside the U.S. Why do such social inequalities exist? Let's examine the two prevailing factors of poverty:

blaming the poor and blaming society. One approach to explain poverty is to blame the bad - that the poor are answerable for their very own poverty. There's some proof to assist this principle because the primary reason humans are poor is the shortage of employment. Consistent with this view, society has masses of possibilities for humans to realize the yank dream, and people are poor because they lack the motivation, skills, or training to discover work.

Some other technique to explain poverty is responsible society- that society is chargeable for poverty. at the same time as it's far proper that unemployment is a first-rate contributor to poverty, the reasons human beings don't work are greater consistent with this technique. Lack of jobs inside the inner town is a primary contributor to poverty. There absolutely isn't sufficient work to support families. Social inequality impacts nearly every measurement of our lives. As an instance, did you realize that children from negative families are three times more likely to die from disorder, injuries, forget, or violence in the course of the primary year of lifestyles than those youngsters born to rich families? Further, on average, rich people stay five years longer than those much less lucky. Politics additionally comply with magnificence lines. Because the rich enjoy the way society is prepared, their wealth tends to encourage them to be extra conservative on political issues, but extra liberal on social troubles. The opposite sample appears to be true for people from poor backgrounds. They have a tendency to be extra conservative on social issues, but more liberal on financial problems, tending to desire government-subsidized social programs that advantage them.

Subsequently, social elegance also impacts family existence. Lower elegance families have a tendency to be larger than center magnificence households (decrease class families tend to marry younger and use less start manipulate). Any other relevant sample is that children from decrease magnificence households tend to be raised to comply with standard values and respect authority. Kids from center and higher elegance families are taught to specific their individuality and creativeness greater freely. There are a few situations that a government professional hinders the rights of a certain person because of his social fame. This case lessens a citizen's dignity as a person, it's just like the officers think that they're better than the civilian due to their role inside the society. An infant's destiny is to be in large part decided with the aid of social repute, no longer brains, I, therefore, conclude that this statement is maximum possibly to be actually given that greater youngsters which have high social popularity grows to be extra a hit that sensible kids that aren't so lucky. This is social inequality.

Social inequality refers to a scenario wherein character organizations in a society do not have the same social status, social elegance, and social circle. Social inequality has many fields including the individual's starting place, man or woman positions, achievements, race, sex, and plenty of greater human beings are labeled in this field and are used to compare human beings and provide popularity to the advanced man or woman. The word social inequality consists of two phrases especially social which refers to a function of residing organisms as implemented to populations people and different animals, and Inequality which means that that several things are not within the equal level or there may be an advanced one from comparing several beings.

Social inequality is also known as social bias, social discrimination, social distinction and plenty of greater. .Social bias can be visible greater often in our USA., we are able to understand that the government is in favor of human beings that have proper social status in place of people inside the decrease magnificence. As an example, some politicians aren't being caught via site visitors' enforcers when they commit a riding violation; that is because of their role inside the society. The guide of the government is biased on the social fame of a citizen. There is no equality, unlucky kids in terrible households' get free training, and unfastened training has a lower best of schooling than private colleges which youngsters with center class families are enrolled into.

Chapter Ten

Learner's characteristics

The phrase gaining knowledge of is used mechanically in discussions about coaching in better training, so it's essential to clarify what we are regarding when we talk approximately learning. Instructional researchers agree that learning is a good deal deeper than memorization and records keep in mind. Deep and lengthy-lasting studying involves knowledge, referring to ideas and making connections between previous and new understanding, unbiased and critical questioning, and the capability to switch knowledge to new and one-of-a-kind contexts.

Studying is a process that:

• Is lively - procedure of engaging and manipulating gadgets, reports, and conversations so that you can construct intellectual models of the sector. Newcomers build expertise as they explore the world around them, take a look at and interact with phenomena, speak and interact with others, and make connections between new ideas and earlier understandings.

• Builds on previous expertise - and entails enriching, building on, and converting existing expertise, wherein "one's know-how base is a scaffold that supports the construction of all destiny gaining knowledge of".

•Takes place in a complicated social environment - and for that reason must no longer be confined to being tested or perceived as something that happens on a character stage.

as an alternative, it's far necessary to think of gaining knowledge of as a social hobby regarding human beings, the matters they use, the phrases they talk, the cultural context they're in, and the movements they take and that understanding is constructed by way of contributors in the interest.

•   Is located in a real context - provides newbies with the opportunity to interact with particular ideas and ideas on a need-to-realize or want-to-recognize foundation.

•   Requires newcomers' motivation and cognitive engagement to be sustained while studying complex thoughts, because huge intellectual attempt and staying power are necessary.

The situations for inputs to mastering are clear, but the system is incomplete without making sense of what outputs constitute mastering has taken region. At the core, studying is a technique that outcomes in a alternate in expertise or conduct because of enjoy. Expertise what it takes to get that information inside and outside (or sell behavioral exchange of a selected type) can assist optimize studying.

Gaining knowledge of is also the technique by using which one acquires, ingests, and shops or accepts facts. The principle characteristic of mastering is a process of acquiring expertise to exchange human conduct via interaction, practice, and enjoy.

•   Characteristics of getting to know are;

•   Learning involves trade.

•   All getting to know involves sports.

•   Learning calls for interplay.

•   Constitute getting to know.

- Learning is a lifelong process.
- gaining knowledge of takes place randomly during existence.
- Gaining knowledge of includes problems fixing.
- Mastering is the process of acquiring facts.
- Getting to know entails a long way more than thinking.
- Revel in is necessary for gaining knowledge of.

Mastering entails exchange

It is a reconstruction, mixed wondering, talent, data and appropriation in a single team spirit system.

As an example, while a baby learns to study they could maintain this know-how and conduct for the relaxation of their lives. It isn't usually meditated in performance. The exchange from the learning won't be clean till a scenario arises in which the new behavior can arise.

All getting to know involves activities

Those activities involve either bodily or mental pastime. They will be easy intellectual sports of complicated, concerning numerous muscles, bones, etc.

So also the mental sports can be very simple concerning one or two sports of thoughts or complicated which contain better intellectual activities.

Studying calls for interplay

At the time of studying, the man or woman is continuously interacting with and stimulated through the surroundings. This experience makes him change or adjust his behavior to deal successfully with it.

Constitute mastering

To constitute getting to know, the exchange need to be everlasting. Transient adjustments can be simplest reflective and fail to symbolize any mastering. Gaining knowledge of is a lifelong procedure. Learning is a lifelong process of gaining and usage the information supplied to someone. It isn't static. Someone in no way stops obtaining new statistics. It keeps someone's mind active and aware however also conscious of the sector around them. Gaining knowledge of happens randomly in the course of life. A few gaining knowledge of occurs randomly at some stage in lifestyles, from new reports, gaining facts and from our, perceptions, as an example: studying a newspaper or looking a information broadcast, speaking with a friend or colleague, risk conferences, and sudden stories. Learning entails problems solving. Learning entails hassle-fixing i.e. expertise and coming across relations among extraordinary contents in a scenario. Mastering is the method of acquiring statistics. Mastering is the process of obtaining data, knowledge, wisdom, and capabilities. It takes place because of interplay with the man or woman's environment. Learning involves a ways extra than questioning. Getting to know entails far extra than thinking: it involves the complete persona – senses, emotions, intuition, beliefs, values, and could.

If we do not have the desire to examine, we cannot research and if we've learned, we're modified in a few ways. If the mastering makes no distinction it may have little or no significance. Enjoy is essential for learning some form of revel in is essential for getting to know. We will get the revel in from direct statement or from formal methods to getting to know which include education, mentoring, training and teaching. We are able to get the enjoyment from direct statement or from formal methods to getting to know which include training, mentoring education, and coaching.

Getting to know is more or less the acquisition of a new discourse, a new way of speaking, appearing, interacting, searching at the sector, and understanding it. It will likely be a hit best whilst the facts received is used and understood. It's a continuous system followed by a man or woman that allows for the purchase of records, attitudes, and practices, thru statements, searching for preceding understanding, looking for publications, and searching within as well as without.

The idea of learner traits is used in the sciences of studying and cognition to designate a goal organization of freshmen and define the one's elements in their private, educational, social, or cognitive self that may affect how and what they study. Learner traits are important for instructional designers as they allow them to design and create tailor-made instructions for a goal institution. It's far expected that through taking account of the characteristics of inexperienced persons, greater efficient, powerful, and/or motivating instructional substances may be designed and advanced. Newbies' characteristics can be private, educational, social/emotional, and/or cognitive in nature. non-public traits frequently relate to demographic facts along with age, gender, maturation, language, social monetary fame, cultural background, and precise needs of a learner group together with particular abilities and disabilities for and/or impairments to mastering.

Adults and gaining knowledge

In relation to mastering, adults are not oversized children. Maturity brings particular characteristics that affect how adults are prompted to study. By way of attractive to the particular characteristics of person novices, we will layout more effective and motivating on-line courses. Here's a listing of generalized traits commonplace to many but no longer all grownup beginners.

• Autonomy. Adults generally prefer a sense of management and self-route. They prefer options and the preference of their getting to know the environment. Even adults who feel anxiety from self-path may additionally learn how to recognize this approach if given a proper preliminary assist.

• Intention-oriented. Many adults have particular goals they're looking to acquire. They choose to partake in learning activities that assist them to attain their dreams.

• Realistic. Adults inside the place of the business decide on practical knowledge and reviews so as to make work less complicated or provide essential competencies. In other phrases, adults need non-public relevance in mastering sports.

• Competence and mastery. Adults want to benefit from competence in administrative center capabilities as it boosts self-assurance and improves vanity.

• Learning through revel in. Many adults choose to research by means of doing in place of listening to lectures.

• Wealth of expertise. In the journey from youth to adulthood, people accumulate a completely unique shop of expertise and studies. They bring about this depth and breadth of understanding to the getting to know state of affairs.

• Practical. Administrative center schooling is frequently part of an initiative that entails change. Adults want to know the motive of education and the inducement underlying an organization's schooling initiative.

• Emotional boundaries. Through enjoyment, adults may

fear a subject, have tension approximately a subject, or sense anger about pressured adjustments in job duties or policies. These emotions can interfere with the studying method.

• Outcomes-oriented. Adults are outcomes-oriented. They've unique expectancies for what they may get out of learning activities and will regularly drop out of voluntary getting to know if their expectancies aren't met.

• Outside obligations. Most grownup newbies have several duties and commitments to the circle of relatives, pals, community, and work. Carving out time for studying influences adult inexperienced persons.

• Potential physical limitations. Relying on their age and bodily circumstance, grownup rookies might also accumulate psychomotor competencies more slowly than more youthful college students and feature more problems analyzing small fonts and seeing small pictures on the computer display screen.

• Big image. Adults require a large image view of what they're studying. They want to understand how the small elements suit into the larger landscape.

• Chargeable for Self. Grownup newcomers frequently take responsibility for their personal success or failure at studying.

• Want for the community. Many self-directed grownup newcomers prefer gaining knowledge of the community with whom they can engage and speak questions and troubles.

In an age where financial improvement is tightly related to better levels of education, the purpose now could be to bring as many students as feasible to the standards required, in preference to focus on just the wishes of the most in a position college students. This means locating approaches of supporting a very wide variety of students with very exceptional levels of capability and/or earlier know-how to be successful. One length clearly does not healthy all today. Dealing with a more and more diverse scholar population is perhaps the best of all demanding situations then that instructors and teachers face in a digital age, specifically but not completely at a post-secondary level. This isn't always something for which teachers ordinarily certified in problem count understanding are properly prepared.

A combination of properly layout and the proper use of era will greatly facilitate the personalization of getting to know, allowing as an instance for different students to work at distinctive speeds, and to attention learning on students' specific interests and desires, for that reason making sure engagement and motivation for a diverse range of college students. however, the first and perhaps most critical step is for teachers to understand their students, and specifically, to identify from the great range of data regarding students and their variations, that are the maximum essential for the layout of teaching and gaining knowledge of in a virtual age.

Some of the characteristics that are believed to be critical from the perspective of designing coaching are:

1. The work and home context

Elements make the work and domestic context an crucial attention in the design of coaching and gaining knowledge of students are more and more working whilst studying (about 1/2 of all Canadian publish-secondary college students also work, and those that do work average sixteen hours every week and the age variety of students maintains to spread, with the common age of students slowly growing (at the college of British Columbia, the common age of undergraduates is 20, but more than one third of all their students are over twenty-four years antique. The imply age for graduate college students in 2014 became thirty-one.

There are several motives for the common age of students increasing, as a minimum in North America:

• Students are taking longer to graduate (in part due to the fact they generally tend to take a smaller have a look at load whilst operating);

• Increasing numbers of college students are going on to Grad College;

• More students are coming lower back for added publications and applications after graduating (lifelong newbies), specifically for monetary reasons.

Partially or completely employed college students, or college students with households, more and more need more flexibility of their analyzing, and especially fending off lengthy commutes between domestic, work, and college. Those college students more and more want hybrid or fully online courses, and smaller modules, certificates, or packages that they could fit around their work and own family life.

2. Inexperienced persons' desires

Expertise the motivation of students and what they anticipate to get out of a path or application must also affect the layout of a direction or program. For educational learning, it is frequently essential to locate methods to transport college students whose approach to gaining knowledge of is first of all pushed by extrinsic rewards together with grades or qualifications to an approach that engages and motivates students in the challenge remember itself. ability college students already with a submit-secondary qualification and a terrific process may not want to work thru a pre-decided set of publications but may need just unique regions of content material from existing guides, tailored to satisfy their wishes (as an instance, on call for and introduced on-line). as a consequence it's far crucial to have some kind of knowledge or knowledge of why freshmen are probably to take your route or software, and what they're hoping to get out of it.

3.   Previous information or abilities

Destiny learning regularly depends on students having earlier knowledge or an ability to do things at a sure level. teachers goal to bridge the distinction between what a learner can do without help and what he or she can do with assist, what Vygotsky (1978) termed the sector of proximal development. If the difficulty stage of the teaching is aimed to a long way beyond the capability or earlier information and capabilities of a learner, then studying fails to arise.

However, the more various the scholars in an application, the more numerous the know-how and talent levels they may be in all likelihood to bring with them. certainly, lifelong beginners, or new immigrants repeating a subject due to the fact their foreign qualifications aren't diagnosed, might also deliver specialist or superior knowledge that can be drawn on to enrich the studying enjoy for all of us. At the equal time, some students might not have the equal basic know-how as others in a course and could need extra help. In this sort of context, it's far essential to design the learning enjoy in order that it is flexible enough to accommodate college students with an extensive variety of prior know-how and abilities.

Virtual natives

Maximum students these days have grown up with digital technologies consisting of cellular telephones, tablets, and social media, which include Facebook, Twitter, blogs, and wikis. Prensky (2010) and others argue that no longer simplest are such students greater proficient in the use of such technology than preceding generations, but that additionally, they assume differently. However, it is especially crucial to take into account that college students themselves vary an extraordinary deal in their use of social media and new technologies, that their use is essentially pushed by means of social and private demands, and their use of digital technology does no longer certainly float across into instructional use. They may use new technologies and social media for mastering though wherein instructors make a great case for it and while college students can see that the use of digital media will immediately assist them in their research. For this to occur though planned layout picks are required on the part of the teacher.

Identify traits of newcomers

Maximum of the scholars at the publish-secondary level will showcase characteristics of "adult learners" and will differ in their motivation and gaining knowledge of patterns from youngsters and young people. For those reasons supplying a gaining knowledge of surroundings that fits the learning desires of your college students has to be based totally at the precise gaining knowledge of forms of your college students' level of educational improvement. As an instance, commonly, person learners:

- Have a more level of adulthood and know-how;
- Bring a wealth of enjoy and prior knowledge to a studying situation;
- Are much more likely to pick out what they need to analyze;
- Decide the quantity to which they may have interaction in learning enjoy primarily based on what they sense is applicable and interesting to them.

Therefore, teaching adults have to:

- Intention to take those factors under consideration
- Take advantage of the grownup inexperienced persons' knowledge and experience
- Be relevant to what they need to study

Traits of mastering patterns

They talk approximately what to do, about the pros and cons of a state of affairs. They imply emotion via the tone, pitch, and volume in their voices. They enjoy listening however cannot wait to get a risk to speak. They generally tend closer to lengthy and repetitive descriptions. They prefer listening to themselves and others communicate.

They generally tend to take into account names however forget faces and are without difficulty distracted through sounds. They experience studying speak and performs and dislike lengthy narratives and descriptions. Auditory rookies benefit from oral practice, either from the trainer or from themselves. They favor to pay attention or recite information and advantage from auditory repetition.

- Like to speak
- Speak to self
- Lose awareness without problems
- Opt for spoken directions over written instructions
- Experience track
- Read with whispering lip moves
- Recollect names
- Sing
- Cannot concentrate when noisy
- Extroverted
- Like listening
- Select lecture and discussion
- Choose verbal reward from teachers

Gear for Auditory inexperienced persons
- Document lectures for repeated listening
- Use rhymes to help memorize
- Say observe material (document and listen repeatedly for assessment)
- Concentrate on recordings of taking a look at material while driving to work or school
- Study aloud
- Talk about the fabric
- Concentrate cautiously
- Sound out words
- Say words in syllables
- Communicate via issues; paraphrase thoughts about new principles
- Paraphrase directions

- Communicate about illustrations and diagrams in texts
- With new techniques, talk approximately what to do, a way to do it, and why it's finished that way

Auditory instructors prefer
- The use of their voices to give an explanation for things
- Recordings, conversations, and call calls
- Dialogue in elegance
- Students to talk about issues among themselves, work together, and contribute their ideas
- Smart use of speech; creating a point nicely
- Argument, debate, and dialogue
- Seminars, institution presentations, student interaction, function plays, and communicate
- To apply the phrases, "give an explanation for, describe, speak, and state" in written examination questions
Methods to interact, auditory inexperienced persons,
- Lecture
- Utilize sound all through lectures
- Use beats, rhymes, or songs to boost information
- Use mnemonic devices
- Ask questions at some point of elegance and allow students to give verbal responses
- Allow students to interact in small institution communication for the duration of elegance
- Use aural cues to alert college students to vital statistics
- Offer verbal summary at the end of each magnificence
- assume, Pair, percentage

Traits of Kinesthetic beginners

They are trying things out, touch, experience, and control objects. Body tension is a good indication of their emotions. They gesture whilst speaking, are poor listeners, stand very close when speaking or listening, and quickly become bored in a long discourse. They recall nice what has been achieved, now not what they've seen or talked about. They decide upon direct involvement in what they are mastering. They distractible and discover it tough to be aware of auditory or visible shows. Hardly ever an avid reader, they'll fidget regularly while managing an e-book. Often negative spellers, they want to jot down phrases to determine in the event that they "sense" proper.

- Move round lots
- Prefer now not to sit down nonetheless
- Move loads even as studying
- Like to take part in learning
- Like to do things rather than read approximately them
- Do no longer choose to analyze
- Do not spell well
- Revel in trouble fixing by using doing
- Want to attempt new things
- Speak with palms or gestures
- Select clothes according to comfort
- Like to the touch objects

Tools for Kinesthetic newcomers

- Stroll even as studying
- Move and lecture the partitions
- Do matters as you assert them?
- Exercise by way of repeating motions
- Dance as you take a look at
- Write words; use markers, pens, pencils to see if they "feel proper"

- Whilst memorizing, use finger to write down at the table or within the air
- Companion a feeling with records
- Stretch
- Write on a whiteboard with the intention to use the gross muscle movement
- Use the computer
- Use hands-on sports with items that can be touched
- Have a look at in quick time durations; get up and stroll around in between
- Make look at gear to preserve
- Use flash playing cards; separate into "know" and "don't realize" piles
- Use plastic letters and magnetic forums for brand new vocabulary
- Write and rewrite to decide to memory

Kinesthetic instructors select

- The use of real existence examples to provide an explanation for things
- Guest lecturers, case studies, sensible work, laboratories
- Well-known shows, samples, running fashions, products, and those that carry reality to the lecture room
- Students to use all sensory modes to offer their thoughts
- Clever use of quotations, metaphors, examples, and analogies in written work
- Demonstrations and open e-book examinations
- To use the phrases, "deliver examples, observe, and demonstrate" in written exam questions

Techniques to engage kinesthetic rookies

- Give breaks while possible and have college students

flow round during those breaks

• Provide palms-on gaining knowledge of gear when possible (models, clay, blocks, and so forth.)

• Use the outdoors for mastering opportunities whilst feasible

• Train standards via games and initiatives

• Have college students answer questions at some stage in class on the whiteboard

• Use dance, play, or role-play sports to enhance records

• Think, Pair, proportion

Characteristics of visible inexperienced persons

They look around and examine the state of affairs. They may stare when indignant and beam whilst satisfied. Facial features are a superb indicator of emotion in the visual learner. They think in pics and detail and feature brilliant imaginations. Whilst significant listening is needed, they will be quiet and become impatient. Neat in appearance, they will dress in the identical way all the time.

They've greater instantaneous keep in mind of phrases that are offered visually. Visible novices like to take notes. Notably unaware of sounds, they can be distracted by visible ailment or movement. They solve problems deliberately, planning in advance and organizing their thoughts by writing them down. They prefer to examine descriptions and narratives.

• Thoughts wander at some stage in lectures

• Observant but may also omit a number of what is stated

• Well organized

• Want to examine and display severe attention whilst analyzing

- Correct speller
- Recollect better with the aid of seeing charts, diagrams, and many others.
- Concentrate nicely
- Need to peer guidelines; now not pay attention them
- Top handwriting
- Right memory for faces however forget names
- Plan in advance
- Not certainly talkative
- Attention to information

Tools for visible newcomers

- Use mind pix or mind maps
- Take notes
- Use "clue" phrases for recalling
- Use colored highlighters to color code texts and notes
- Use maps, charts, diagrams, and lists
- Watch audiovisuals
- Take photos
- Use take a look at playing cards or flashcards
- Use notebooks
- Watch trainer's mouth and face
- Use visible chains or mnemonics
- Watch television
- See elements of phrases
- Write down guidelines

Visual word instructors decide upon

- The usage of written textual content to provide an explanation for matters
- Email
- To present handouts and count on the class to have study broadly and well
- Smart use of phrases as well as the usage of interesting

words
- Argument and discussion in written shape
- To location vital phrases at the board or overhead
- Setting words in some order, such as using priorities or categories
- Lists of factors and matters in vertical and left-aligned arrangements
- Texts that are dense with text, summaries, and abstracts
- Not to apply more than one choice questions, until the appropriate answer depends on discriminating among phrase meanings
- To use the phrases, "define, increase the case for, justify and analyze" in written examination questions

Visual picture teachers decide upon
- The usage of visuals to give an explanation for matters
- Net pages that have sturdy photographs, warm bins, and so on.
- Diagrams, slides, charts, graphs, arrows, circles, and containers
- Complicated thoughts to be shown first in a diagrammatic version
- Crucial phrases and ideas to be located on the board so that they're spatially thrilling as opposed to left-aligned arrangements.
- Texts which can be dense with diagrams, graphics, color, and white area
- Videos
- To apply the words, "illustrate, show, define, label, link and draw a distinction among" in written examination questions
- Their college students to visualize and notice the point

Techniques to engage visible newbies

- Write out instructions
- Use visuals whilst teaching lessons, which includes pics, charts, diagrams, maps and outlines
- Bodily reveal duties
- Arrange facts using shade codes; preserve color codes regular
- Deliver college students the opportunity to put in writing notes in the course of the class
- Use visible cues to alert students to important information
- Provide pattern questions for college kids to jot down out the answers or have students use diagrams to answer questions
- Provide written summary of lesson on the end of notes/lecture presentation
- think, Pair, share

The characteristics of the learner are as varied as any personal traits, however, the HSC PDHPE syllabus has exact five (5) which you should recognize nicely. These traits of a person have an effect on their potential to and velocity at which they research a new talent. The characteristics can consist of character traits, inclusive of a willingness to study and receive grievance. They also encompass hereditary factors, which include your peak or body kind. Self-belief stages can even have an effect on the price at which a new skill is learned. An athlete ought to now not be over-confident, but neither ought to they lack self-belief as both are averse to talent gaining knowledge of. Other characteristics of the learner including their prior studies and herbal potential will even affect the ability to get to know. An athlete with fine stories in learning abilities, in particular, similar skills, will research new competencies faster. As will an athlete who has top notch natural ability such as the individual that obviously has good hand eye co-ordination.

- Traits of the learner, e.g.
- Persona
- Heredity
- Confidence
- Earlier experience
- Potential

Scientists and psychologists have advanced some specific models to recognize the unique ways that human beings research first-rate. One popular principle, the VARK version, identifies four number one types of beginners: visual, auditory, studying/writing, and kinesthetic. Each studying type responds fine to a one-of-a-kind technique of coaching. Auditory newcomers will don't forget information nice after reciting it lower back to the presenter, even as kinesthetic rookies will jump on the hazard to participate in a hands-on pastime.

Every presenter that stands up in front of a target audience desires to be understood. However, whilst your target market is ready to study fine in relatively one-of-a-kind methods, how do you ensure which you get your message across to everyone in the room? The effects of those learning styles reach some distance beyond the lecture room. In case you need to educate a big organization of people, no matter what the placing, you need to recognize how to interact with each of the four gaining knowledge of patterns.

Happily, there are a few easy matters you could do as a presenter to make sure you're catering to every sort of learner on your target audience, whether or not you're speaking to loads of webinar attendees or thirty coworkers in a small schooling consultation. Check the infographic beneath, or hold analyzing to study greater approximately the VARK version's four number one studying patterns and what you may do to interact them all for your next presentation.

It's essential to increase lesson plans to assist all of the one-of-a-kind varieties of beginners absorb statistics in a way that fits their man or woman desires. When instructors understand the traits of various gaining knowledge of patterns and associated education techniques, they may be better able to deal with the academic necessities of all their students.

Because every pupil learns in another way, studying patterns are widely recognized in each classroom management principle and the educational concepts in well-known. "The term 'mastering patterns' speaks to the understanding that window. Technically, a character's gaining knowledge of fashion refers to the preferential manner wherein the pupil absorbs, strategies, comprehends and retains information," train.com explains. As an instance, one scholar may research first-class via appearing a process out, at the same time as any other might decide upon studying approximately the subject as a substitute.

The VARK version
The gaining knowledge of kinds of college students depends upon numerous elements, such as their

surroundings and other cognitive and emotional factors. Because each scholar is distinctive, it's an awesome idea for instructors to expand lecture room strategies that contain distinct getting-to-know patterns for one-of-a-kind types of inexperienced persons. The VARK model helps teachers try this. It's far an acronym that refers back to the four getting-to-know patterns: visible, auditory, analyzing/writing preference, and kinesthetic.

VARK is targeted on the concept that scholars retain and procedure records in a different way and have "favored getting to know modes" that allow them to study their high-quality. "Permitting college students to get entry to facts in phrases they may be cozy with will increase their instructional self-assurance," teach.com explains. It's crucial to observe that, while absolutely everyone makes use of a combination of learning patterns, most have a clear preference for one opens in a new window.

Understanding gaining knowledge of styles

* Visible

Visible newbies opt to take in information the use of charts, maps, graphs, diagrams, and greater. Using images to give an explanation for principles and ideas is a nice way to attain a visible learner. But, this type of gaining knowledge of fashion does now not consist of pics or motion pictures. As a substitute, visible newcomers learn best when records is supplied using styles, shapes, and different visual aids inside the area of written or spoken phrases. One way instructors can differentiate their training for visual beginners is by using the usage of graphic organizers to train a lesson. A glide chart is probably used to provide an explanation for a systematic technique, for example.

• Auditory

This gaining knowledge of style describes college students who analyze high-quality whilst statistics is heard or spoken. They benefit from lectures, institution dialogue, and different techniques that involve speaking things. "Regularly humans with this desire want to kind things out by means of speaking first, rather than checking out their thoughts and then speaking," VARK research limited explains. To assist auditory freshmen to examine, instructors can put up audio recordings of classes at the magnificence website, or include group activities that require students to provide an explanation for principles to their classmates.

• Analyzing/Writing desire

Students who've a reading/writing preference opt for records to be supplied using phrases. They love to study and carry out nicely on written assignments which include tales or e book reviews. "This preference emphasizes text-based enter and output – studying and writing in all of its bureaucracy," VARK research restrained notes. A high-quality way to assist these students to analyze is by means of having them describe diagrams or charts using written statements. Then, they could take a look at their notes later to better hold the records.

Kinesthetic

Kinesthetic rookies examine fine while they could use tactile stories and perform a physical hobby to exercise making use of new facts. "Folks who pick this mode are linked to truth, 'both through concrete private reviews, examples, exercise or simulation,"' VARK examines restricted explains. Give these college students a living proof of a concept or procedure, or mission them with recreating experiments to demonstrate ideas.

Understanding the way to deal with the mastering wishes of your college students is an vital a part of growing meaningful lecture room studies and assisting them retain what they study. To research extra about techniques for special newcomers, check out our direction, Differentiated practice. It gives instructors the know-how and equipment to devise practice that reaches a wide range of rookies. With this path, you could have interaction students and effectively differentiate learning for higher consequences.